You Can Go Home Again

A Career Woman's Guide to Leaving The Work Force

By:
Pamela A. Piljac

871865
Bryce-Waterton Publications
Portage, Indiana

Library of Congress Cataloging in Publication Data
Piljac, Pamela A., 1954-
    You Can Go Home Again: A Career Woman's Guide to
    Leaving the Workforce
    Includes index

ISBN 0-913339-03-2

Printed in the United States of America

This book is dedicated to my husband, Thomas, for all his help, understanding, inspiration and support.

Other books by Pamela A. Piljac:

- The Bride To Bride Book
- NEWLYWED: A Survival Guide to
  the First Years of Marriage.

About The Author

Pamela Piljac left her career in financial management to experience life as a homemaker. She pursued her lifelong dream of being a writer, and is the author of THE BRIDE TO BRIDE BOOK, and NEWLYWED: A Survival Guide to the First Years of Marriage.

Acknowledgements

I would like to thank those who contributed their ideas, assistance and support to make this book possible, especially Florence Zavacky, Barb Krga, Jennifer Pielow, Linda Sims and Laurie Grace. All the names attached to stories in this book have been changed.

Table Of Contents

Preface

For the past twenty years women have been struggling to enter the workforce. Why would I write a book to guide women who are leaving their jobs?

I belong to a new generation. We finished school, started our careers and got married, just as we were expected to do. We planned to work all of our lives and we seldom considered staying at home. It wasn't a viable option for today's woman. Life as a homemaker has been portrayed to us as a drab, dreary and boring lifestyle. The thought of trading my hard won successes for the virtual anonymity of a housewife may have been a fleeting temptation at the end of a hectic day—but that is all it was. I admit that there were times when I wondered what it would be like to sleep when I pleased, or to have the time to enjoy my interests without other demands pulling me away. Yet the thought of becoming dull, and dependent on my husband was more than enough to push the thoughts from my mind.

Since then I have discovered that this image was wrong. I want to share what I have learned with other women who have always worked, and help them to decide if the decision to stay at home would be right for them. I want to help women who select this new lifestyle to make the difficult transition from career to home as smoothly as possible.

I made the decision to leave my career in the midst of a corporate shakeup. Jobs, offices and employees were being realigned and reassigned. I was offered three different jobs located in three different states. None of them appealed to me. Yet, I knew that if I turned them down I would kill my chances for future advancement. It seemed like an ideal time to step back and re-evaluate my future goals. I decided to resign from my job. Still, the decision was hard to implement. I found myself wavering often in the last few weeks, especially as I made my final goodbyes. But the promise of freedom and extra time for myself sustained me. I left my job and became a homemaker.

The change in lifestyle was abrupt. One day I was the manager of a multi-million dollar operation with employees, reports, and awards on the wall. The next day I was just another housewife at the supermarket. I wanted to shout "There's more to me than you think!" to everyone I saw. As I slowly adjusted to my new life, I began to develop fulfilling interests that I barely had time to think about when I was working. I began talking to other women, and was surprised to discover that the stereotypical housewife that I had seen in the media no longer existed. In fact, many of those other women were professionals who had also left exciting careers. Why did they leave? For many reasons—to improve their marriage, to have more time with their children, or to make a different life for themselves. But the overwhelming consensus among them was that although it wasn't easy to leave their career, they were glad they did. None of them planned to stay away from the workforce forever. But they wanted two, five or ten years to try a different lifestyle for themselves.

This book is based on extensive research, as well as my own and other women's experiences. It is meant to help you begin a new life. As Henry David Thoreau once said: "Why should we be in such desperate haste to succeed, and in such desperate enterprises? If a man does not keep pace with his companions, perhaps it is because he hears a different drummer."

Introduction

No matter how fulfilling your job is, there are times when you wish there was less struggling and juggling needed to make all the pieces of your life fit together. It is difficult to find a workable balance between your career and your personal life without compromising one or the other. One week you must give up time you would like to spend with loved ones in order to complete an important project at work. The next week you cut out time that you should devote to your job so that your private life can receive more attention. Sometimes it seems that you are powerless to control the never-ending cycle. After all, what are your alternatives? Is there any other way to combine your own needs with your family's so that everyone is happy?

There is. You can experience life as a homemaker. With the right attitude and preparation you can continue to grow, thrive and be an energetic and intellectually stimulating woman. You can enjoy the same benefits that you obtain from your career, as well as the freedom and extra time that staying at home will give you.

The homemaker of today is a new breed. She is a pioneer for her generation who enjoys the creativity and independence that her lifestyle allows. She has examined the benefits of a career, but opted to spend at least part of her life away from it. It isn't always easy for her—life as a forgotten and maligned minority can't be—yet she believes that the benefits far outweigh the costs.

"You Can Go Home Again" describes the circumstances that shaped the attitudes that women share today. It insists that women should not be locked into any role, whether it is as a homemaker or a career woman, but that all women should feel free to experience both choices. It will demonstrate ways to make the transition from career to home with a minimum of frustration and anxiety. It deals honestly with the problems that can occur and provides insights for overcoming them.

There are suggestions to help you adjust to living on a reduced income and ideas to help you maintain independence in your marriage without having the clout of a salary. There are sections that provide guidance for re-examining your identity and methods for setting future goals.

As a woman today, you deserve the best possible life for yourself and your family. You need to take the time to evaluate what your options are, and how you can pursue them. *"You Can Go Home Again"* will help you to find a way.

SECTION ONE

Making The Decision

You Can Go
Home Again

Today we scoff at the deluded housewife of the 1950's. "How could she have done it?" we puzzle. Why did she sacrifice herself in the name of everyone else's expectations? We easily criticize this past generation, but these women were only doing what was expected of them. The books, magazines, radios, newspapers, and talk shows in those days all offered her the same helpful advice. To fulfill herself and her role in society, she must marry, have children, and put the cares and concerns of her husband and children before her own. If a woman chose to avoid this lifestyle, she received either pity or disdain from her peers, and her social life was often in limbo. The pressure on all women was tremendous, and in the end the housewife rebelled.

Today's women enjoy an incredible number of choices in their lives. They are told that they can fulfill themselves and have a happy home life by balancing the frustrations they feel at home with the rewards of a career. They are offered helpful advice on how to climb the corporate ladder with one hand, run a happy home with the other, and find personal growth and satisfaction at the same time. The pressure on women has been tremendous, and the cracks in "super-woman's" role have been apparent for some time. Now, women are searching for a new lifestyle that will allow them to integrate everything that is important to them, as well as the time and the freedom to enjoy it all.

We have begun to recognize that feelings of self-worth and

accomplishment do not necessarily come from a career. Simply accepting that the sparkling home in the suburbs should be replaced by the briefcase as the new sign of success can be as damaging to us as was the 1950's myth that each woman had to marry and have children to be fulfilled.

For the past twenty years the role of homemaker has been considered an unusual and old-fashioned lifestyle. Women who choose this role are often made to feel unintelligent, foolish, and dull—when anyone bothers to pay attention to them at all. Despite this attitude, some women are leaving the workforce. They are tired of fatigue, disillusionment, and a battered personal life all in the name of success. Frustrated by the unrealistic expectations placed upon them, they struggle with the confusing battle between following the status quo, and understanding their true desires. Feeling different from their peers, they ask themselves "What's wrong with *me*?"

A new sense of camaraderie has dawned as women slowly have begun to admit to one another that although a career can be exciting, there are times when it is as much fun as a rainy day with all of the children at home with the flu. Ready to defy the media's message that to have it all, you must do it all', these women are finding individual solutions to their goal of combining self-fulfillment with marriage and motherhood. Once they take the courageous step to the role of full-time homemaker, they are often pleased to discover its rewards. There is almost a pioneer spirit to the feeling of breaking new ground for their generation; and bringing new attitudes and goals to a formerly traditional lifestyle. Many assert that since 'someone will find a way to criticize you no matter what you do, you might as well live the way that you please'.

The decision isn't as easy for every woman. To walk away from a career somehow diminishes you in the eyes of your peers. Often frustrated by the attitudes of others, new homemakers often want to shout "I haven't changed—my attitude toward life has changed!" In addition, our mothers are often the most emphatic supporters of our pursuing a career. With admonitions to "avoid a life like theirs", and tales of ambitions that they would have followed if they had the same opportunities, it is no wonder that we find it hard to see life at home as worthwhile. Yet, staying home today is different than it was for our mother's generation. No woman is expected to sacrifice her life for her family today. Every woman can have several different lifestyles if she chooses—some years pursuing a career—other years enjoying her home. Most importantly, our mother's generation often romantically fantasized life as a career woman. You and I know both the rewards and the realities first hand.

Making a major decision is never easy, and with too many choices, our goals and deepest desires can become confused. With new opportunities continually arising, and a barrage of voices offering advice, we feel guilty if we do not try out as many opportunities as we can. We are all a little bit frightened of change. To step away from the security, power, and well-worn path that we are so familiar with, is a big risk. There is no guarantee that taking such a risk will give us more than we had before. To be a homemaker requires an enormous emotional investment. You must focus your time, talent, and energy on a lifestyle that is often unadmired, and seldom appreciated.

The freedom to live your life as you wish is worth the risk of making a change. Those courageous women who dare to be different have the strength that allows them to carve out a new life in whatever way they choose.

Women Who Leave

A small group of highly motivated, educated, and successful women are leaving their careers. They are at the forefront of a trend that could gain momentum at any time. They are tired of dashing through life and trying to stay one step ahead of the competition steadily pursuing them. They decided to resign from evenings of rushing home through traffic to an equally tired family. They said 'enough' to family time spent in arguments over who should have started dinner or called the repairman. After the excitement of breaking new barriers in the workplace; and the exhilaration that comes with power, money and prestige; came the discovery that their job is also a grind of company politics, ethical tradeoffs, and disappointments. Here are a few of their stories:

Joyce

"I came to the conclusion that making it in a man's world meant hiding my own feelings and emulating theirs. I resented having to fit myself into the male mold. I was tired of having to constantly guard my business-like image. The final straw was a company gathering where a few of the wives present were homemakers. They tried to be friendly, and I know they couldn't understand why we corporate women had to avoid them like the plague. The thought of being caught chatting with them about something inconsequential was terrifying. It could have permanently damaged our chances for respect at work. I decided that this lifestyle was too phony for me, and got out. Now I can be myself, and talk to whomever I please, whenever I please. I have made my life just as invigorating as it was when I advanced in my career, but now I have the freedom to enjoy it."

Danielle

"As I advanced in my career, I watched many women struggle to decide if they should have children or not. They knew that once they returned to work after maternity leave their chances of promotion would be damaged. The price of having a child seemed tremendous, and some couldn't take the chance. Their only hope was that the rewards in their job would be worth the loss of never having children. I concluded that any lifestyle that is that demanding and precarious, couldn't be as important as I had thought. I wasn't sure if I wanted children, but if I chose to have them and a career I would have to work three times as hard to prove myself because I was not only a woman—I was a mother. I decided to have a child and give up my career. I plan to work in the future, but in my own business, where I am the only help or hindrance to my advancement."

Becky

"I enjoyed the prestige that my job brought, and my salary allowed us to have many of the good things in life, The funny thing about a career is that you quickly become caught up in its demands, and at times you find yourself putting tremendous importance on things that are crucial to your work, but of little consequence to the rest of the world. I had a report to gather on all of our affiliates, and I worked day and night for a month to get it done, I missed my son in his first play, and my husband's award dinner. I wanted the report to be excellent, and it was. I expected it to make a great impression and waited for some indication that it had. Then my boss mentioned that nobody ever bothered to read it. I felt like I had been run over by a train. Here I was sacrificing my life, my marriage, my children, and my values so that I could say "yes, I am working, and I'm successful at it". I know now that I can make it in a man's world, and that's enough. I decided that I didn't need my career any more. I have to admit that I miss the extras—but the price is more time to enjoy my life. I'm worth it!"

Karen

"A job can be exciting. There is nothing more gratifying than doing the impossible well, then being rewarded for it. But it can also be boring. There is nothing worse than listening to the same drones sing the same song at every meeting you attend. Maybe I expected too much from my job. Athough I advanced at a reasonably impressive rate, each new step seemed a little emptier for me. When you think about it, no matter how important you are, a job is simply work that you are paid currency for performing. How could that be 'the answer' to happiness?''

Sarah

"I slowly developed this perspective. I could work hard for twenty or thirty years, and hopefully acquire plenty of power and influence along the way. If everything went as planned, I could be at the top of my industry, with all the rewards and esteem that it would bring. In the mean time, I would have little time or energy for a personal life. It would mean limited true friendships, and hours spent with people I cared little for to 'cultivate' my advancement. It also occurred to me that I would have little to look forward to once I reached this pinnacle of success. I decided that what I might become in the distant future was not as important to me as the person I could be along the way. I want to enjoy my life as it happens, not live it for future possibilities. I chose to leave my career and make my life with my family. So far, I have few regrets.''

Connie

"When we women were leaping into the workplace to follow the same path as the men—why didn't we look harder at where we were going? We wouldn't have had to look too closely to realize what their lives were like—we had seen it in our own homes often enough. They worked long hours and had little time for their personal lives. They spent their lives polishing an image, and gearing for the next move up the corporate ladder. Each increase in income brought an increase in items of prestige necessary for their position. In the end they may have attained success, but they often lost their families along the way. Why didn't we say 'who needs life on a treadmill' instead of rushing out to join them? I know, I'm as guilty as the rest. I was just as eager as everyone else to prove that I could be a person of importance and consequence in the workforce. But at least I can say that I was smart enough to quit while I was ahead!''

Jill

"We were told that we could be anything that we wanted to be. How can you walk away from that kind of opportunity? I worked my way through business school, then acquired a job at an investment brokerage firm. I never thought about staying home after I married, or even after my son was born. This was the role I was expected to fill—exciting career woman, wonderful wife, and loving mother. When the thought of leaving first occurred to me, I pushed it out of my mind, thinking it was a temporary fantasy. But it grew stronger and I seriously began to consider the possibility. I finally decided that it was a lifestyle I wanted to examine more closely. Believe me, it took a lot of courage for me to say 'I want to stay home!' My friends still don't believe I am serious, and keep insisting that I'll go back. Perhaps I will someday, but that's in the future. Right now, I'm still adjusting to life as a homemaker. I haven't decided what to do with all the free time that I have, but I'm sure that I will soon.''

Sharon

"I landed some of our agency's biggest accounts, and was top saleswoman for three years. I won awards and trips, and dined with millionaires. It almost seems bizarre to follow that with 'right now I prefer Cheerios and Dr. Seuss'. They certainly aren't as glamorous, and some people may think I am crazy, but my children are very important to me right now. Their childhood won't last very long, and I want to enjoy those years while I can. When they are over, I'll start a new career. I know I can succeed again.''

Cathy

"Five years of working at a highly respected firm, then they folded. I had worked hard so that my future could be secure, and instead it's shakier than ever. My skills are valuable, but there are few companies in this area that could utilize them. In order to work in my field I would have to relocate. I've decided to become a homemaker instead. Just as our mothers counted on marriage as their security, we depend on our careers. The truth is that nothing in life is very secure, so why not enjoy it while you can? I can work again in the future if I want to, but being home with my husband and children has made our family life more relaxed and pleasurable. I want to be a part of it as long as I can.''

Renee

"I was working too hard. I felt like I was losing control of my life and everything began to overwhelm me. I was constantly irritable and tense, and began to have trouble sleeping. I found myself avoiding people—every contact seemed to make more demands on my time. One day, in a fit of rare anger, I said 'I quit' and typed my resignation. I stunned everyone, including myself. They have offered me my job back, but I don't think I'll take it. I want to spend some time thinking about the future, and it's wonderful to have as much free time as I like every day. I'm not ready to give that up again.''

Valerie

"To be blunt, I was burned out. I was tired of dealing

with the same problems year after year. Job burnout is fairly high in my field, the solution is usually to move up when it starts to occur. But I had seen my co-workers move up and face a whole new set of problems that I didn't find attractive. I had lost my enthusiasm for my career, and no longer cared if I advanced or not. I stopped giving 100%, and some days I barely did anything at all. I have always had a great deal of pride in my work, and I decided that if I couldn't do the job well, I shouldn't be doing it at all. Although it meant a tremendous cut in income for us, after talking it over with my husband, I decided to leave. Now I'm giving my best to my husband and family.''

These women discovered that their needs were not being met. Unable or unwilling to change the system, they instead decided to withdraw. They turned their backs on expectations and demands that were no longer appealing, and are willing to experiment until they find the best balance for themselves and their families. This small underground delights in their rebellion, and in the freedom that it brings. Ready to accept that there is more to life than simply self-gratification and extra income, they have discovered that the more they are able to give to their lives, the more they receive in return.

Making Your Decision

There's a good chance that you have considered leaving your career, but aren't sure if the decision would be the right one for you. You can begin to further examine your attitude by writing out the pros and cons for leaving and staying. Your list might include the prestige, money, and personal satisfaction that you gain from your career on the positive side; and the frustrations, loneliness, and fears of life as a homemaker on the negative side. Then ask yourself: What need does your job fulfill in your life? Does it give you your only means of control, recognition, satisfaction, self-respect or purpose? Is it your outlet for creativity? Are most of your friends and social contacts through work? Can you meet those same needs as a homemaker? How do you respond to the thought of staying home? Does the possibility excite you? Frighten you? Are you unsure what your feelings are? Here are some of the dilemmas that other women have faced:

Carolyn

"On the one hand, by leaving my career I would be dubbed a 'flash in the pan' by my co-workers . . . as someone who could succeed in the short term but not over the long haul. I've seen it happen to other women who left. This attitude could affect my opportunities for resuming my career in the future. In addition, I would have to attend my class reunion next year and say that I was a homemaker. I used to joke about women who were homemakers, so they would probably think that I had had a nervous breakdown and was covering up. On the other hand, I would love to leave work and have the freedom to do what I wanted to every day. It would be wonderful to spend time with my children without feeling guilty about not having more of it. It would be so nice to be able to go away with my husband without the tremendous juggling of schedules that requires now."

Sally

"Who doesn't think about the pleasures of staying home? You could sleep in during blizzards and dash to the beach on beautiful sunny days or spontaneously decide the way that you will spend your time. How often do you get to do something impulsive when you are working? But how could I give up the income that I bring in? It would seriously affect our standard of living and I'm not sure that I could be happy struggling with the bills every month. What if I didn't like it and wasn't able to resume my career? It's a tremendous risk."

Donna

"At first I thought that daydreams about leaving my job were an escape mechanism—something to help me to deal with frustrations after a trying day. After a time I realized that it was something that I would like to try, but I was afraid to take the step. I don't have children and staying home seemed almost silly. I didn't have an excuse and my only reason was that I wanted to. After five years of college and five years working hard to reach the level that I did, it seemed almost immoral to stop."

Vicky

"I never seriously considered leaving until my second child was born. I realized then that I had been giving my first child what little free time that I had; and with a new baby, something had to give. To top it off, it seemed as though most of my income went to the babysitter and cleaning service. Giving up my career wasn't easy, but I couldn't see having children and then paying strangers to raise them. I had to make a difficult choice, but my children are worth it."

Sue

"One day I walked out of our company headquarters at eight o'clock at night and thought 'I can't remember the last time I have seen daylight. Was it a week ago? A month ago?' I didn't know. I stumbled in to my cave during the gloomy morning hours and emerged in the dark of night. I started to think about how tired I was of working. Sure, I made a decent salary and had a company car. But I was fed up with pointless memos, boring meetings, business lunches and company picnics. I didn't want to bother with networking—I was tired of getting to know people just so I could use them at a later date. When it came down to it, no one part of my job had the lure and excitement that it once did. I considered changing jobs, but I knew that ultimately it would be more of the same. I decided to take a vacation. Maybe I just needed time to revitalize. My husband and I talked about the possiblity of my leaving and he was very supportive. He felt that I was working too hard and he really wanted more time for us to be together. ''I can't tell you what to do'' he told me ''but it might not be a bad idea to go back for a few weeks just to make sure.'' My routine at work seemed even more dreary and tiresome after my vacation. I submitted my resignation. Today I am taking my time and considering other options.''

Vanessa

''The idea of staying home seemed both wonderful and terrifying at the same time. I couldn't bear the thought of having to ask my husband for money. And what if I somehow lost myself in my husband's and children's lives? It seems like that could happen so easily. How would I spend my days? Shouldn't I be doing something more important with my life? Would being a housewife make me dull and lazy? But it's a very tempting idea. Freedom, peace, no more guilt, plenty of time to rest and relax. It's the riskiest, most challenging career move that a woman can make.''

Ellen

''Now I can admit that I used my children as an excuse to leave. I was tired of my job, and had reached a professional plateau. I could either launch an all out drive to move up—or throw in the towel. I bought the towel. It was easier and somehow more acceptable to say that 'my children needed me', rather than 'I am tired of working'.''

Julie

''Most women today can't abandon their jobs simply

because they would like to. We work for personal fulfillment and to maintain a higher standard of living. In many cases, leaving a career would mean giving up a source of self-esteem, and total disruption of the lifestyle that we have become accustomed to. We would have to struggle more, worry more, have less, and be able to do less. To be a homemaker today is a luxury. How would the children get through college? Would we have to stop traveling? Where would I find the money to redecorate the house, or buy nice things? Husbands today are not as willing to be the sole breadwinner either. They resent the pressure of complete financial responsibility, and enjoy the comforts that an extra income brings. To become a homemaker requires a tremendous examination of your values."

Lynn

"In a job, you are only as good as your last success. Your superiors are primarily concerned with what you can produce for them; and your co-workers with how they can step into your shoes. No one cares if you are satisfied, if you raise wonderful children or if you make your husband happy. Of course you can't really expect them to, it's not what you are being paid for. I didn't have to make a choice—but I did. It seemed easier to select one or the other to focus my energies on, and I chose my family."

Nancy

"I was a working mother, and it's a hectic, demanding, frustrating life. You miss so many important firsts in their life, and even if you pretend that it doesn't hurt, or that the latest success at work makes it easier, it really doesn't. I always knew deep inside, that sitters just couldn't give my children the same love and attention that I did. When I finally confronted that feeling I decided to resign from my job. I'm not saying life at home is perfect either. In fact, it's a hectic, demanding, and frustrating life in different ways. But I wouldn't trade places with another working mother for anything.''

Tricia

"I loved my job, but once I had my baby it was so hard to leave her. She seemed so helpless! I found myself thinking about her all day long. By the time I arrived home I was so exhausted, and I would only have about an hour to spend with her before she fell asleep for the night. I began to feel like I wasn't achieving my goals at work, I barely knew my child, and my husband was a passing stranger. It still took alot of thought, but I left my career and became a full-time wife and mother.''

The truth is, you do not need a career to give you feelings of worth and satisfaction. You can be a homemaker and remain mentally stimulating, healthy, and interesting; and develop a fascinating social life too. Your success depends upon the commitment and effort that you put into your life as a homemaker.

Once you have determined your own needs and your willingness to withstand the loss of income or negative opinions of others, break your final decision into steps.

1. Imagine your life as a homemaker realistically. Mentally take yourself through a day.
2. If you can, take a vacation. Live each day as close as possible to what your daily routine as a homemaker would be.
3. Discuss your plan to leave with your husband and children. How do they feel about it? Will they be supportive?
4. List all of the possible negative consequences of your

change. Face each one directly. Then ask yourself, what is the worse thing that could happen? Confront and deal with it.

Having It All

It's realistic to assume that you will not remain a homemaker for the rest of your life. You may enjoy your time at home for the next two, ten, or twenty years, but at some point you will want to or need to return to work. A single lifelong pattern in one role or another is no longer viable today. Because we have so many paths and choices available to us, and because our needs vary during different periods in our lives, it is more sensible to examine the tradeoffs and payoffs in each stage, and live accordingly. By finding a way to fulfill your needs during each phase, your life will entail a greater overall feeling of satisfaction and achievement. In summary, you can enjoy having a career and be a homemaker too, if you are willing to do it in a series of connected moves.

With thought and creativity many women have found ways to utilize their skills differently and have successful second careers. Remember, there was a whole generation of housewives that descended on the work force in the early years of feminism. Many were able to apply or develop the knowledge they gained as homemakers into proof that women could be successful in many different fields.

Your final choice depends upon your priorities. If being at the top of your profession is your primary goal in life, and absence for any period of time would obstruct that goal, then perhaps you shouldn't leave. But if you are willing to search for other channels of success, you will be able to spend time as a homemaker and still enjoy a career.

When You Have No Choice

Not everyone leaves their career because they freely choose to try a different lifestyle. Company closings, layoff, an inability to relocate, realignment of positions, or being fired can all leave you a homemaker without prior planning. Being told that your services are no longer required is always painful no matter how sweetly the words are packaged. Yet, it is not that unusual for achievers to be let go at one point or another in their career. Until now it may only have happened to other people, and you reassured them by pointing out all of the successful men and women who were fired and went on to achieve greatness. Once it happens to you it might be more difficult to identify with such stories.

Most people have an inkling that they are going to be fired or laid off long before the axe falls. If there weren't broad hints or indications of corporate problems; you may have been aware deep down that your performance at this particular job was not up to par. Perhaps you were bored and apathetic because you weren't being challenged. If you are aggressive and independent you may have forgotten to make your boss look good. Or you may have been one of the millions of people who work at jobs that they are completely unsuited for. The real reason may not be immediately evident as you deal with your initial emotions. Being fired can make you feel numb, incompetent, isolated and betrayed. A few other women share their stories:

Jan

"Our industry hit a downward spiral very quickly. One day I was enjoying a thriving career, the next I was out of work. The company had pared itself to a skeleton workforce, and there was no indication of if and when the rest of us could return. With the whole industry hurting, the few job openings available meant competing with hundreds of others. Many of them had more experience and more prestigious credentials than I had. The jobs that were being offered were at a lower pay with fewer benefits. It was definitely an employer's market.

Because I had never planned or prepared to stay home, it was a tremendous adjustment. We were hurting financially—we had just bought a new home. My husband was a nervous wreck worrying about the payments, and it didn't ease the situation for me either. I had never realized how much of my identity was tied to my career. Suddenly I felt like a non-person, a failure, and unable to control my life. I continually asked myself: 'Why hadn't I seen it coming? Why did we buy this house? Why hadn't we saved more? Why didn't I develop more skills that would be transferable to other industries?' I was angry at everyone and everything.

After a few months of agony and of nearly destroying our marriage, we were able to gain a better perspective with the help of a counselor. We were so afraid of losing what we had we were letting possessions control our lives. It still wasn't easy to let go. We had this feeling of taking a tremendous step backward in our lives. We decided to sell our home and some land that we had purchased. Surprisingly, it brought a feeling of freedom as well as relief. My husband's income is more than ample for us now, and I think I would like to stay home for a few more years. I would like to strengthen myself, and our relationship, so that no job loss or financial crunch will ever harm us so deeply again.''

Gail

''One day our Senior Vice president called me into his office. 'Gail' he told me, 'You've done a great job here. You've taken over our auditing operation and you've streamlined it so well that it's going to be a model for our other departments. We really appreciate the hard work that you have given us here and I know you will perform equally well on your next job.' It took a moment before I realized I was being fired. 'Why?' I asked him. We've decided to combine your position with someone else's and he has more seniority. I know you'll understand, and of course you can count on a top-notch recommendation from me."

I felt as if I had been shattered into a million little pieces. In spite of the fact that my performance hadn't caused the problem, I still took it very personally. Although I knew that these things happened, I had never had anything like this happen to me. I received good grades in school, was never in trouble, and always received excellent evaluations from my employer. Now I had been fired.

I went home and called my husband. He tried to console me as best he could, but one thing about being fired is that you suddenly feel very alone and vulnerable . . . no matter how much reassurance you may get. I was devastated, and for a while I withdrew from everyone. I didn't want to get out of bed in the morning, much less consider looking for another job. With that much time on your hands, sooner or later you have to start thinking. I realized that I was being foolish to let the fact that I had been fired by a company that was notorious for economizing affect me so deeply. I also concluded that I deserved more than the rigid program I had set for my goals. I began to re-evaluate myself, my needs, and my ideals. For the first time in years I had a chance to think about my future, and those thoughts have brought many changes. I'm planning to start my own business soon and I'm very excited about the ideas that I have."

Has anyone told you that being fired was probably the best thing that could have happened to you? Given you the pep talk that now you can gain a new perspective on your life? It may be irritating to hear at first, but it's true. At first you will feel shock, anger, bewilderment and perhaps self-pity. During those days you may be tempted to consider a few actions that would be utimately self-defeating. They include:

- Slandering your old boss or your old company.
- Hanging around your former workplace as often as possible.
- Telling everyone how you could have improved things if they would have given you the chance.
- Trying to convince other employees to quit.
- Taking revenge by destroying property or reputations.
- Asking yourself such contemplative questions as "Why am I here?" "What is life?" (You are too vulnerable for that kind of thinking at first.)

Instead, concentrate on the benefits of leaving your job. Here are a few to consider:

1. You will have time to learn more about yourself.
2. You may discover new insights into your career goals and work habits.
3. You can expand your interests and consider new options.
4. You will have more time to share the lives of those you are close to.
5. You can utilize your different talents to find new ways for satisfaction and fulfillment.

When you you are asked to leave a job there is often pent-up anger and frustration that is buried inside for a long time. Some women are able to channel these feelings into creative energy to succeed elsewhere, while others let it gnaw away at them and ultimately suffer even more. Whichever type you are, it may help to follow this two point plan to revitalize your energies:

1. Sit down and write out everything that has upset you about this job loss. Why was it unfair or wrong? List all of the ways the company made mistakes. How you could have done it better. Don't forget the

stupid and petty things that they did. Read it over. Are you satisfied? Did you forget anything? Once you have gotten it off your chest, tear up what you have written. Don't show them to anyone, no matter how clever they sound. You don't want your words coming back to haunt you some day. Another benefit of this exercise is that it may help you to rediscover your original goals and principles.

2. Do not allow yourself to become passive. Force yourself into taking part in activities that require mental stimulation. Design your dream house. Paint a picture. Don't give lethargy a chance to take over.

Your New Life

Although women can often choose to stay home if they wish; it still takes courage to see the risks, know the difficulties, and select a life as a homemaker. Many women uncover new power and abilities and a satisfaction from transforming a home and a lifestyle into an atmosphere that they and their loved ones can enjoy. Life at home can be a wonderful period of growth and an opportunity to be the person that you have always secretly hoped to be. Women who stay home often marvel at how much this lifestyle can improve the way that they view life and the way that they live it. They usually become closer to their husband and children and find more happiness in those relationships. They have discovered a way to create an oasis of sanity in an unordered world.

Transitions and Tradeoffs

Evolution

There have been times in our history when the barometer of success was measured by the amount of time a person could spend in leisure activities. People that could spend their days as they pleased, who could enjoy education, travel, music and literature had the esteem of their peers. In other eras, work became the standard for evaluating an individual's worth. The more a person could acquire the more he was revered. During these periods work often became the focus and purpose to life, and any activity that was unproductive was deemed unnecessary.

If we examine life in our century it becomes apparent that these two attitudes alternate in a continuing cycle. In some periods it is necessary to work hard to obtain the things that are wanted or needed. When they are acquired the attitude toward work eases. There is a desire to find ways to secure goods without working as hard. Free time and leisure become highly valued, and new methods are devised to profitably exploit what has been earned. It is time to buy a nicer home, or to redecorate the one you already have. You may purchase a lakefront cottage, vacation in Europe, or simply pursue your favorite activities and enjoy life as a family. As this desired quality of life becomes the norm a new restlessness takes over. It is time to make improvements on what we have and create a better life for the next generation. There is a good example of this cycle when we examine mid-twentieth century life:

During World War II the economy was booming. Factories couldn't keep up with demand and jobs were plentiful. Farmers could sell whatever they produced. Women were working, men were fighting, and everyone was earning money but had few available goods to buy. It was also a difficult period. Families were separated, men were dying and most items in everyday life (such as sugar and gasoline) were rationed. When the war ended, people wanted to enjoy life. The family, leisure time and a home became the American dream. By the 1960's a new restlessness took over. People had acquired what they wanted and enjoyed the benefits. Now they wanted more. As the baby boom generation reached adulthood it became easier for women to enter the work force because there were more people demanding goods and services. More workers were required to produce them, and as women began working they spent more money on daycare, clothing, entertainment and other items which generated even more jobs. With more dollars chasing fewer goods the inevitable result was inflation. Suddenly everything cost more. It was now necessary for women to work just to maintain what they had already acquired. For many families their spendable income deteriorated from "Should we take a three-week cruise?" to "Can we take a vacation?"; or from "Will we be able to make the house payment?" to "Can we have meat for dinner?" In order to keep what they had or have any chance at all of getting ahead, it became essential for the family to have two wage earners. Such a necessity becomes easier to accept when it becomes widespread in a society. Today, both men and women are measured by their productivity. The more they can acquire, the more admiration they receive from their peers.

The Role Of Women

Until recently men and women lived out their lives in clearly defined roles. They knew exactly what to expect, and exactly what was expected of them. The man was the protector, the woman was the child bearer. The man was the provider, the woman was the keeper of the home. Each worked hard and depended on the other to supplement the family's needs. Even if a woman did work outside the home, that role was secondary to her job as wife and mother.

These attitudes are intertwined with the new role of women in the workforce. Her economic contribution to the family and the power and prestige she has attained has put her in a different position than women of past generations. In addition to 'child bearer' and 'keeper of the home' she also shares the now dual role of provider with her husband. Because of this additional contribution she looks to her spouse to offer assistance in the care of the home and children. Although men are helping more than ever before, it is still rare for them to contribute equally.

It became the job of today's woman to do it all—a career, a home, and a family—by finding a precarious balance between the three. Out of this struggle 'Superwoman' came into being. She was shown as an ideal, a woman who could have the best of both worlds. It worked out wonderfully for everyone. The standard of living could be maintained and there was a potential for a better future. The pressure was off of men to be sole providers and now they could enjoy their families more. Until the facade began to crack, no one seemed to wonder if it would ever end. Then women began to ask themselves "Why me?" "Why am I the one who has to do it all?" "How do I know that I can't obtain satisfaction and fulfillment at home since I'm never there?"

Revolution

How did women get to that point? It all began simply enough. Although men wielded the power in the world and were able to make the decisions that affected their lives, women decided that they were now going to have a say. After years of struggle the woman's movement gained strength and momentum. They were determined to find a way to allow their special nurturing and caring qualities to

have an impact on society. They began their biggest campaign for the right to vote. Once acquired, they hoped to use
the power of the ballot box to end wars and other evils in
society—after all what woman would vote for a man who
wanted to send her son to a battlefield? They were notable
sentiments, but having the right to vote wasn't enough and
they knew it. Their next ideal was for women to achieve
positions of power in the higher echelons of business and
government. Perhaps they were ahead of their time, or
perhaps they didn't understand the esteem that most
women felt for the institutions of home and family. Whatever the case, the movement fizzled and the cause for
advancement of women lay dormant for many years.

The American housewife was part of the American dream.
She had a home in the suburbs, a station wagon, children
and a dog. She was a part of the leisure period that followed
the second world war. At that time she was told how to
think, act, feel and believe. For many years she remained
trapped in her role, sublimating her own feelings to meet the
standards that were expected of her. But she had the
opportunity to reflect on her frustrations and re-examine her
values. When Betty Frieden captured the hidden anxieties of
these women in her book "The Feminine Mystique" she
touched a hidden nerve. Women rallied together in response
to the realization that they were not alone.

The women's movement rose again to help women
understand the choices they had, and to better utilize them
in the world around them. Rather than support women at
home by providing alternatives for their problems, the new
movement told them that they required freedom *from* their
home and family *to* maintain a job outside the home. This
was the prescription for fulfillment and prestige. At a point
in our social development when families needed each other
more than ever; when we should have been doing everything we could to place a higher value on humanity because
we lived in a world on the brink of destruction; women chose
to leave their homes and put the lives of their families on the

back burner for the new 'cause'. Their justification was that after years of oppression they deserved the opportunities for themselves.

Like all minorities striving to assimilate into society the women worked together to develop a strong self-image and sense of direction. They encouraged one another to take advantage of every opportunity and fight for more. They descended on the work force with the same plan that other minorities had used: "If you can't beat them, imitate them."

The success ethic that these women wanted to participate in was one that men had been following for years. It went like this:

- Your function in life is your job.
- Your job title and salary are your worth.
- The combination of the three determines your status.
- You are your job.
- Therefore, the way to develop yourself is to acquire a job that will provide the most prestige.
- You then have a label to prove your value and establish your identity to others.

Men had followed this ideal but they had never been able to succeed in getting all of their satisfaction from their jobs. Those that tried inevitably ended up with a troubled personal life and the feeling that they had lost themselves along the way. It hasn't worked for women either. In addition, the women have had to work twice as hard to establish themselves in positions of importance. Surveys of professional women indicate that they work longer hours at their jobs than many men, while they continue to do most of the work around the home. Most women still consider themselves happy in their careers—but of course they have little time to think about their happiness because they are too busy trying to be a perfect wife, mother, homemaker and executive.

In short, women today have escaped from the boredom

and loneliness that housewives once felt into the prison of anxiety and false values in the workplace. In a time when men were in need of change, when our own special qualities were more important than ever before, we began to emulate the men instead of changing them.

Men's Liberation

The woman's movement had a tremendous impact on men. Their roles were shaken. Their word was no longer law. No one was there to greet them with their pipe and slippers when they came home.

Once their initial disgruntlement began to fade, men began to notice the benefits of the new woman. She was happier because she could live her life as she pleased. She was contributing to the family financially so there was less pressure on him as provider. While the couple struggled to make their relationship more equal, the man began to re-examine his values. He wondered "Am I fulfilled?" "Am I in a trap?" "Is this worth it?"

Men began to claim that they too, wanted freedom from oppression. That they no longer wanted to be 'just a meal ticket' for the family. That they were tired of marching into fixed and established roles, and that they wanted the freedom to explore new interests. They wanted to ease the expectancies that they work, produce and succeed their entire lives and spend more time with their families.

Transitions

Clearly, men and women were moving in opposite directions. Women have begun to define themselves by their jobs, men have begun to explore other avenues of fulfillment.

There was a catch to all this for today's woman. She now had two packaged lifestyles to choose from. With one, she could stay at home and care for the children, husband and home. She would receive no admiration or reward, have less money and less clout in the relationship. She would be seen as hurting the family's chances for a better future. Or she could go to work, put the kids in daycare, have more money, more clout in the relationship, still care for the home and have no time for herself.

We must bear in mind that both men's and women's roles are still in transition. It is difficult to judge what the end result will be of our struggle. On the one hand a woman in the next generation may find it easier to leave her children and go off to work. She might feel less guilty than we do because she never lived in a traditional lifestyle, and you can't miss what you don't know. On the other hand there may be a backlash to the women's movement. Home and family are still important to most people, and unless more value is placed on them, the pendulum may swing away toward less freedom of choice for women. Ideally, the women in the next generation will have employers that are more co-operative with the demands of raising a family by allowing flex time, shared jobs or encouraging work from the home.

There are four questions we must now ask ourselves:

1. Did women over-react to the powerlessness that they felt when they pushed aside the strengths they had and indentured themselves to the male success ethic?
2. Does a world under constant threat of nuclear annihilation really need to encourage more people to be aggressive?
3. Should a society where people have become alienated and self-centered discourage a lifestyle that values the home and family?
4. Can women change the world with their basic qualities of care and giving, and successfully turn men towards those ideals instead of becoming 'little men' themselves?

Women don't necessarily know the answers. There are still many barriers to break before they can truly say that they have the power to affect society. There are still many justifications for their acquiring positions in the workforce by imitating men. They have to start somewhere and they do.

But there is resentment among us. The older women who overcame the obstacles and obtained equality believe that the younger women do not appreciate what they have done, and are too quick to forget what still remains. They are right. It is difficult to imagine what life must have been like when women were trapped as housewives. It is easy to believe that now that women have jobs they will never have to worry about equality again. It is almost human nature to ignore issues that aren't glaring.

Younger women resent the fact that the women's movement raised the questions without having answers. They feel it's unfair that they be offered choices that are loaded with other problems. Yet the movement had to begin somewhere. And we never want to go back to the days when there were few acceptable alternatives in women's lives besides wife and mother. We must be careful that a retreat from the disillusionment of trying to have it all does not become a retreat from equality itself.

Often when it is impossible to control the world around us we look for answers elsewhere. We hope that someone, somewhere, can tell us what to do. There is no way to evade the complex issues that women are confronted with. There are no easy solutions.

The answer to personal happiness lies within. This does not mean that you should make a cult of your self, but rather that you examine your deepest values and needs. You cannot be satisfied or have a direction in life if you don't know who you are or where you are going. Once you find the answers it is not the end. It is not time to go out and look for ways to gratify yourself. It is time to begin to grow in new directions, to understand that a job, title, power, cars, homes, clothes and jewels will not make you what you are. Only you can do that. The cult of self in the 1970's didn't solve problems, it just created new masks for people to hide behind.

The answer is not to retreat from equality, but to equalize our lives. Women should pursue career interests and gain all the satisfaction and fulfillment that can be had. But they should also feel free to leave the work force and experience life as a homemaker if they wish. The homemaker today is the true beneficiary of the women's movement. She has the training, background and freedom to choose her lifestyle. When she does choose to stay at home it is because she wants to, not because it is expected of her. She discovers different challenges and opportunities than she had in the workplace, and can use them as vehicles for personal growth.

However, society is reluctant to acknowledge her intangible contributions. In our hurry to destroy the stereotypical housewife, we also extinguished the pride we should feel for the millions of women who care for their families and create loving homes every day. They are left alone in a wilderness with their intelligence questioned and their contributions unacknowledged. In our haste to accept today's career woman blazing new trails on the job, we allowed ourselves to develop a condescending and biased attitude of any woman who does not slavishly adopt the same lifestyle. Prejudices are based on ignorance. Those who think that they are better than women who stay at home are only demonstrating their inability to break away from popular assumptions and create their own conclusions. Many housewives believe that such people are not really callow, they are jealous. There is a valid point here. As stated in a *Parents* magazine survey (7/83) "while 29% of jobholders indicate that they are never envious of full-time home-makers, 57% say they are occasionally envious. These occasional twinges of envy are attributable to their perception that (homemakers have) more freedom (50%) . . . (and) more rewarding lives (12%)."

All women are first-class citizens and each should have the freedom to choose the contributions she wishes to make. As the economic difficulties begin to ease we will once again look for ways to enjoy what we have earned. We will want to create a better quality of life and enjoy the company of our loved ones. We will once again esteem our home, children and family. When we do, the women who had the courage to try life as a homemaker will be at our forefront as role models for a new generation of women who can have a career and be a homemaker without fear of scorn.

SECTION TWO
Being A Woman Today

Career Today

If you had been born in the latter part of the 19th century you might have taken a job as a teacher, secretary clerk or factory worker. Your income would have been used to support yourself or your parents. If there was any extra money available you would have tucked it away to save for special items you wanted to include in your hope chest. Sooner or later the day would come when you agreed to marry. No matter how much your income would have helped the family budget or improved your standard of living, you were expected to quit your job. It was time to devote yourself to your husband and begin a family.

As a young woman in the 1950's you might have opted to continue working after your wedding day. It would have been accepted that you and your husband had decided to set aside some extra money for the future, or perhaps for a home in the suburbs. However, once you became pregnant with your first child you were expected to submit your resignation. It was time to concentrate your energies on your husband and family for the rest of your life.

We have come a long way. Women today expect to work all or part of their lives. Futurists predict that by the end of this century only one in ten women will never have worked. Surveys of this new generation of women show that they see a career as a vital part of their future happiness (Mademoiselle 10/82). There are over 50 million women working today (U. S. Labor Dept.) and their reasons for working are as varied as their individual personalities. For some it is an economic necessity. For others, it is a means of independence or personal satisfaction. Three determined career women share their reasons:

Celia

"I love my work. Sure there are difficulites at times, but the benefits far outweigh the drawbacks. I think that the happiness and satisfaction that I get from my job helps me to be a better wife and mother. I especially enjoy the many luxuries my income allows us to have. For example, I hate housework. I don't want anything to do with it, and if I wasn't working you can be sure that my home would be in permanent disarray. Now I can pay someone to do those chores and spend my days doing something else. My income gives us an opportunity to travel, which we had always dreamed of doing. We have been able to take the children to Yellowstone and the Grand Canyon and Yosemite. I know that the trips were educational for the children and I also hope that they helped to enrich their appreciation for the world around them. But that's not all. I think that my lifestyle will help my daughter prepare for her future. She can see first-hand that it is possible to balance a career and a family. To me, this example is the best legacy that I could give her."

Hillary

"I think that the self-sufficiency that I have gained through my career helps me to have a better relationship with my husband. He isn't the source of my identity, and our marriage isn't restricted by the demands that my dependence might bring. We can meet each other on equal ground as two people who can succeed on their own but want to share their lives through marriage.

My job has also been an enormous source of personal

growth. I have learned to overcome prejudices and command respect for my abilities. It is never easy for me to keep my temper in check, but I've learned to maintain my composure when someone wrongfully attacks my ideas. I've overcome misery when my most cherished plans were defeated. I found ways to come back and persevere until my goals were implemented. I've learned to draw on my inner resources when it seemed that the last drop of my strength was gone. Although I've proven my worth to others, I have discovered that the most precious reward is the value I place on my accomplishments.''

Rita

"Until my husband lost his job we had a very traditional relationship. He paid the bills and I cared for our home and family. Although we discussed any decisions that had to be made, we both believed that his word was final. About one year ago the company that he worked for was bought by a major conglomerate. Most of the middle management was let go and my husband was devastated. He lapsed into a terrible depression and nothing I said or did seemed to help. He made no effort to find another job, so after weeks of watching him sprawled in front of the television I went out and found a job of my own.

I wasn't sure what his reaction would be. I knew that he had lost his confidence and that the idea of my supporting us would hurt him even more. Yet, someone had to pay the bills! He became even more miserable and dejected and after another two months of dealing with his resentment I finally convinced him to seek counseling. In time he snapped out of his lethargy and eventually found a good job with another company. He then informed me that he expected me to resign my position so that our lives could 'return to normal'.

I couldn't. It was as if I couldn't trust him anymore. I had lost faith in our implied agreement that he would always care for us. I knew that I never wanted to be that dependent on him again, and that I wouldn't be helpless as long as I could count on my earnings. I also like having my own income. We are able to save more and I can buy things that I would like to have for our home, or for myself and the family. My husband still doesn't like it, but that's the way it's going to be."

What Do Working Women Face?

You've gained economic clout. You've made significant advances in the struggle for equality. You've attained positions of power and prestige. And you've done it while you shifted between roles of wife, woman and mother. It isn't easy to find a balance among these roles or to be sure which represents what you truly want from your life. Each role is defined by a set of values that you, your family and society places on them. Sometimes it seems that women have ended up with the worst of both worlds.

Let's play a game. There are two sets of quotations here. Read them and try to describe the person that is speaking:

#1 "My personal life is a disaster. The demands of my career are tearing me apart. My problem is that I want it all. I want to be the best in my field and I want happiness at home. Instead I am working a twelve hour day just to keep my head above water. My marriage is falling apart and my kids are like strangers to me."

#2 "I often feel frustrated . . . "
    "I feel alone most of the time . . . "
    "I am usually bored . . . "
    "So much of my work seems pointless . . . "

Did you guess? The first quote was a male executive—did you identify with it in any way? The second consisted of phrases excerpted from statements made by happy and successful career women—did it sound a little like the stereotypical housewife? To be fair, let's finish their sentences:

- "I often feel frustrated by the many demands on my time."
- "I feel alone much of the time because I am the only woman executive in our sector."
- "I am usually bored with the many meetings I must attend."
- "So much of my work seems pointless to my husband, but it is important to me."

What I want to illustrate is the fact that the problems you face today as a career woman are a composite of those faced by men and women throughout the years in their traditional roles of provider and homemaker. Career women are trapped between two powerful institutions—the family and the corporation. According to Betty Friedan: "If a woman tries to have it all work, complete with slavish adoption of the male pattern of success where you drive your whole identity by the scores in the rat race and at the same time go home and take the main responsibility for the children and home according to the patterns of women in the past . . . she's going to be in trouble." (Chicago Tribune 6/13/85)

It shouldn't be surprising that the once glamorous image of career women has begun to fade. The hidden frustrations, the effect on her personal life, and the dangers of burnout are being discussed in the media. The long erratic hours, inflexible routines and dashed expectations have sent many women searching for other ways to obtain happiness.

Going home is not the answer for every woman. There are no either/or choices or Utopian lifestyles that will make life simple for you. What *is* important is selecting the best way for you to live at different stages of your life. If you are tired of what you are doing or questioning its value, then it may be beneficial to take a sabbatical from your career and re-evaluate your goals. If you are honest with yourself, you'll realize that you wouldn't be reading this book if you weren't at least considering a change of lifestyles.

When You're
A Mom Too

"Since 1950, the number of mothers who work outside the home has nearly tripled" (*U. S. News & World Report*, 8/6/84). More women than ever before are trying to raise healthy and well-adjusted children while struggling with the responsibilities of a career. Most mothers who work outside of the home believe that they are doing what is ultimately best for their family. They enjoy the fulfillment of a career, their children benefit from the material things that their salary can provide, and they believe that the extra effort that they put into their mothering will make up for the time the children must spend without them. However, most mothers who stay at home believe that a full-time mother is what every family needs; that a woman can be fulfilled without a career; the children would be better off with a mother's constant care; and that a working mother can never make up for all of the hours that she spends away from her children.

No matter how tolerant they try to be, each side secretly believes that the other is wrong. What all mothers must understand is that like religion and politics, mothering styles are a matter of personal conviction. In truth, each group would like to have some of the benefits that their counterparts enjoy. Working mothers inevitably dream of more free time to play with their children. Homemakers often fantasize about having more time of their own to communicate with other adults and receive recognizable rewards.

Does it make a difference if the mother works? Many agree

with the conclusions of Dr. Jacqueline Lerner, a psychologist at Penn State. In her study she tracked 100 mothers for 28 years. Her purpose was to find a "direct connection between adjustment in a child and a mother's employment status." She found that "The most poorly adjusted children were those with mothers who wanted to work but were staying home and those with working mothers who felt they really should be home" (*McCalls*, 5/85).

Although it makes sense that happy mothers will raise well-adjusted children, the problem for many mothers is the guilt and worry they feel no matter which route they have taken. One woman explains her feelings:

Irene

"I haven't found the perfect answer. I like the added income from working, but when I am putting in such long hours there is little time for me to enjoy the money. I know we buy too many things for our children—there are times when I am afraid that we have become 'Disneyland' parents. Yet we want them to have the best of everything, and it's hard to deprive them of anything we can provide.

I also must consider my own life. What will I do after the children are grown. If I'm already in the midst of a thriving career when they go off on their own, I am less likely to suffer from an 'empty nest' depression. But the other side of me says 'What if your children get into trouble while you are busy building a career? Wouldn't you be the sorry one then?' I know that I could resume my career after they are grown, but I just can't make a decision. I receive a great deal of satisfaction from my job and I love being with my children. I do believe that my daughters are more independent than they would be if I was home all of the time—but sometimes I'm afraid that this is making them grow up too fast. There have been times when they have needed me, and I've had to comfort them by telephone. How can you ask a child to put their pain on hold for eight hours? That's a lifetime to them. A friend of mine told me that it is more important that I be a good role model so my daughters will feel free to reach for their goals. I agree, but I wonder if a mother plagued with guilt and ambiguity is the best role model for her daughters?"

Irene could examine both sides of the issue realistically, but she couldn't reach a conclusion. Here are a few other women that have strong opinions—yet you can't help but wonder if they are doing the right thing either.

Deanna
"I don't want my children raised by someone else. Yet it has been very hard for me to enjoy staying at home. I'm tired of messes. I am bored with crying children. I don't want to spend my days fishing tiny cars out of the toilet and wiping up spilled milk. I want to get dressed. up in the morning and walk out the door. I want to spend my days at a place where no one says 'mommy' and everyone appreciates what I do. Some days I have so little energy that nothing gets done. The house is a mess and dinner isn't started when Joe gets home and the children have spent half the day in front of the television. Other days we play together and everything goes well. I just can't seem to find a balance, but I know that this is what I must do. At least my children will know how much I care."

Mona
"The idea that my children need my full-time attention is utterly ludicrous. Why *should* I be at home waiting for them when they come home from school? If they have something to tell me, they'll share it later. In the mean time they'd rather be playing with their friends. Children today don't need constant attention. They are more sophisticated and savvy about the world

and they don't need a mom hanging around dropping sugary platitudes. I'm raising my children to be tough because that's the way the world is. No one is ever going to smother them with love and attention and they might as well learn it while they're young."

The Case For Staying At Home

Several women shared their feelings as to why they believe it is important that a mother stay with her children full-time. You will find a more detailed discussion of the case for staying at home in the chapter called "Homemaker".

Tina

"Your children don't listen to what you say as much as they watch what you do. If you are seldom there they may not remember to question things that puzzle them, such as your telling them it is wrong to steal and then bringing home office supplies. Or they may turn to someone else—a babysitter, their peers, television—for their answers. That is why I believe that full-time motherhood is so important. If my daughter has a question or a problem about something she sees or hears, I am right there on the spot to help her understand. You can't pass your values on to a child be seeing them for a short period every day and telling them right from wrong. They have to see you doing it right before they can imitate you."

Carmen

"I can't believe that a woman who works full-time during the first years of her child's life will develop the same close relationship as a mother who was there all day and every day. A child needs to feel secure and close to his mother when his personality is forming and if she is only there part of the time, how can that feeling develop as it should? The trouble is, if she has always worked she won't recognize the difference. If she has any rapport with the child she will consider that 'closeness' to be the same thing. She'll never know the tight, intense bond that we full-time homemakers feel, and that is so terribly sad."

Linda

"What frightens me is the children today. So many are experimenting with drugs in elementary school, running away from home and even committing suicide. Many women believe that this only happens among the poor, but it is also happening in upper-middle class and well-to-do families at an alarming rate. Those children are the future leaders of their generation and they are growing up with serious problems that money alone can't repair.

I know that such tragedies can happen in any family whether the mother has a career or not. Studies show that a mother working outside the home has no affect on the way the child turns out, but what if we find out in twenty years that these studies were wrong? personally, I think it is more than a remarkable coincidence that more children are getting into trouble at the same time that more mothers are working outside the home.

I think the real problem is that so many mothers see what they want to see in their children. They can't believe that Johnny or Susie could do anything wrong. Although some homemakers have this attitude, it seems to predominate among the career women that I know. In fact, I can always tell which children in the neighborhood have mothers that work. The children either spend most of their time at my house soaking up the family atmosphere or they are what I call 'Eddie Haskell' types, real smooth and polite on the surface but troublemakers underneath. They learn early how to manipulate their parents, and usually mom and dad have no idea there is anything wrong until the child has a real problem. My message to working mothers is 'How do you really know what Johnny and Susie are up to when you only see them for a few hours every day?'"

Jean

"Our roles as mothers are multi-faceted, and communicating with our children is just one small part of the job. Children are constantly encountering new things, they are always looking for answers, and more than anything else they need a place that gives them a feeling of love and warmth at all times. We are there at home to create a special place, share the special moments and give our children roots and stability. I can't help but say to all working mothers—if you didn't want to stay at home with your children, why did you bother to have them? They are not toys to be taken off the shelf and played with when you feel like it. They are real live people, and if you brought them into this world you should make sure that you are there for them."

Carla

"You know your children better than anyone else and only you can pass on your heritage, values and interests. What if you work for all of those years and give them the best schooling, the most expensive clothing and all the other extras, then discover that you set such a materialistic example that those are the only things that your children really care about?"

Alicia

"I'm tired of hearing about quality time. So many working mothers smugly say that because they focus their undivided attention on their children for an hour or so each day it is just as valuable as time spent with a full-time mother who is distracted with other things throughout the day. That is bull. For one thing, all of your time with your children should be quality time. I can't believe that giving your child an appointment for your attention can be equated with a mother who is there and who can be interrupted from her other chores if necessary. My children don't understand quality or quantity, they just know that I am there for them whenever they need me."

Ann

"A friend of mine tried to tell me that her child was better off with her working because stay at home mothers just sit in front of the television all day. I couldn't help but laugh. Although I'm sure there are housewives who do spend all their time watching television (just as there are career women who seldom have time for their children), what did that have to do with her son? He was the one being affected by her not being there, not some other child in a different family. And what on earth does she think most babysitters do? The ones that give your child constant undivided attention are extremely rare and valuable. Anyway, I asked her "If you stayed at home would you watch television all day?" "Of course not!" she said. "What would you do?" I asked. "I don't know, I guess I would spend most of my time playing with Bobby" she answered. "Then please explain to me" I asked her "how your son is better off with you working instead of you playing with him at home?" She didn't have an answer, but I think I hit a nerve because she has barely spoken to me since then."

Jackie

"Right before I had my baby an older woman executive pulled me aside. "Are you planning to stay home and raise your child?" she asked. "Well, for a few weeks" I told her. She was one of the smartest and most respected women in the firm and I was flattered by her interest. "Listen" she said. "I worked full-time for all the years my children were growing up. If I could do one thing over it would have been to stay home and treasure every minute." I was too surprised to say anything, so she went on, "You don't believe that you would enjoy it, but believe me there are always careers you can pursue . . . but you only have one chance to be with your children. Your life with them is what you make it, and if you are as smart as I think you are you can keep yourself up and raise a family at the same time." "I'm afraid that I would resent my children if I was with them 24 hours a day" I told her. "Of course you will be frustrated" she told me. "But don't make the mistake of counting the days until they're out of diapers, then until they start school and so on. Remember, each day is really one day less that you will share your life with them on such an intense level. Don't give it up any sooner than you have to." I thought a great deal about what she said and in the end I did opt to stay home (it's also what my husband had wanted all along). But I do think that every mother should ponder what she said, children grow very fast—and you can never replace those years."

Child Care

The biggest headache most working mothers have is finding good and reliable caretakers for their children. The best are often quite expensive and difficult to find. However, these mothers have ambivalent feelings about babysitters that usually fall into one or more of these categories:

1. If the babysitter is terrible I am afraid of the affect that she will have on my children.
2. If the babysitter is too good I am afraid she will replace me in my children's hearts.
3. I resent my babysitter because she is always there for my children and I am not.

4. I am not sure I could be a good mother full-time, so the children are better off with someone who is qualified to care for children.

Realistically, a mother can never be replaced by a babysitter in her children's eyes, no matter how attached they become to that person. Mothers who are insecure must understand that no one—no matter how expert (even Mary Poppins herself) would be better for *her* child than she would be.

Mothering

Perhaps you are uncertain whether your children would be better off if you stopped working. Here are a few questions to ask yourself:

- Am I living by the same values that I want my children to follow?
- Would I want my children to emulate the same lifestyle that I have lived?
- Do my children feel secure in my love?
- Are they learning to be sensitive to a world beyond themselves?
- Do they care more for other people than for materialistic things?
- Am I honestly guiding them through life?
- Do they feel wanted, loved and cared for?
- Am I accessible enough to discuss their problems with them?
- Am I teaching them compassion for others?
- Will they be strong enough to withstand the worst of peer pressures?

If you can answer yes to these questions, then you are probably on the right track in raising your children.

Should you decide to become a full-time mother there are several adjustments that you and your children will make, and three pitfalls to watch and prepare for. They are:

Impatience: It is much easier to be patient with a child that you see for only a few hours each day. In addition, when you are working, mothering is a change of pace from your full-time job and may seem more like play. As a full-time mother you must devise ways to enjoy your child's continuous presence and still maintain your composure.

Super-parent: Highly motivated and dedicated women are accustomed to taking on a challenge then trying to be the best. They dash straight into full-time motherhood wanting to bake cookies and share every possible moment with their children. Because the children have been relatively independent until then, they may be confused by the extra attention that you are giving them. It is better to slowly ease both yourself and your children into these new roles.

Overload: To justify your being a full-time mother you may feel that you need to be needed. You are not the only one who can do things for your children, nor are you totally responsible for your family's emotional and physical well-being. If you try to be all things to your family all of the time—you will end up tired, frustrated, resentful and depressed.

There are no perfect mothers. A child needs a mother who values herself, shows that she cares, and helps them to grow into responsible adults who display all of the qualities that our society holds in esteem. Only you can decide the best style of mothering to generate these results in your family.

When You Don't Have Children

It is highly unusual for a woman to give up her job to stay at home when she has no children. She must suffer even more disdain and disparagement at the hands of her still employed (and now jealous) friends and acquaintances, than do homemakers who are also mothers. She is made to feel as if she is lazy, non-productive and not contributing anything with her life. She is thought to be foolish, or a person who is unable to succeed in the workplace. She is asked to doubly justify her decision and lifestyle to everyone she meets. In short, it isn't an easy role to fill.

A few other women share their stories:

Monica

"My former boss wouldn't believe that I was planning to stay home. 'What would you do all day?' he asked. 'I'm not sure' I told him, 'but I know I want to give it a try.' He was convinced that I was going to work for a competitor. He kept laying traps trying to catch me. He was so positive that I couldn't stay at home that he called me from work seven times during the first week I was gone. When he finally realized that I was telling the truth he became very upset. 'You're wasting your talents. If you don't have children your duty is in the workplace.' It was very strange—I mean I didn't work there any more and it wasn't like we were saving the world with what we had been doing. I worked in the corporate headquarters of a major department store!

His attitude typifies what I had to deal with. My own mother doesn't understand why I prefer to be a housewife. She went to work when I was still in high school and was one of the first female managers in her company. She thinks I've taken a giant leap backwards for woman-kind. I was good at my job, but I didn't like what I was doing. I went to college and started working just as everyone expected me to do. I want to take time and think about my future.

I don't know if I want to have a baby, or stay home alone, or start my own business, or try a whole new career. But now I have the time to talk to other people about what they do, or go to the library and research some of my ideas. My mother thinks I'm being selfish but I don't think that's true. I have a lot of years ahead of me and if I am going to be a good wife, daughter, friend or mother I need to know myself and what I want. And the happier I am with myself, the happier I can make other people.''

Roxanne

''It's frustrating because most people assume that you have children. I shop in the same grocery store every week and naturally I shop alone. Yet whenever I buy candy bars the clerk always hands them to me and says 'I know you'll want to put these in your purse so the kids won't see them.' Since she's only trying to be helpful I don't bother to correct her.

Whenever I meet someone new and they discover that I don't work or have children—they don't know what to do with me. I think they assume that I must really be dull if I have given up the two most popular roles for women. Sometimes I get so tired of it that I want to make up a tragic story as to why I don't have children just so they will feel guilty for asking.

I like my life and I don't consider myself useless. I love my home, I have a happy marriage and I have other interests. For one thing, I take an elderly neighbor to the doctor every week and run other errands for her. I also do volunteer work at our local hospital one day a week. My life is full and satisfying without children or a career. I can't help it if other people can't understand that."

Marcia

"I wanted out of the rat race. When you are a woman who doesn't have children you don't dare turn down a business trip or a request that you work weekends. Any inkling my boss might have had that I wanted more time for myself or my husband would have been proof to him that I didn't have the 'fire and vigor' to make it to the top. But having a super-career just stopped being important to me. It was a gradual feeling of dissatisfaction that I was finally able to identify. One day I broached the idea with my husband. To my surprise he was enthusiastic. He felt we needed more time together, and because he travels a great deal he thought it would be wonderful for me to be free to accompany him. We have been able to visit many different states and several areas in Canada. It is almost like our lives are one long vacation.

I've learned to ignore stupid comments people make when they discover that I don't 'do anything'. We have a very happy life together. Some day we may have children—but I don't need them or a job—to justify my choices in life."

Claudia

"I left my corporate job eight years ago. I didn't have any children and I didn't know if I wanted them. I just knew that I wasn't happy in my career. My time at home helped me to learn a great deal about myself and my marriage. I discovered that I had inner resources that I had never drawn upon before. My marriage became one long honeymoon with dinners by the fire and champagne breakfasts. Every day I would take a long walk along the river near our home and marvel at the peace and serenity that I found there. On one of those walks I decided to return to school and get my teaching certificate. One of the things I enjoyed the most about my previous job was training other employees. I also felt that I could offer a lot to my students because of the business experience I had acquired. I did teach for three years, but then lost my contract due to budget cutbacks. Although I enjoyed teaching I also missed my time at home, so I decided not to look for another position. There is such a tremendous freedom in doing what you wish, to follow your impulses. What I love about my life is that I can select the way that I live it one step at a time."

Abby

"Every day for ten years I headed into the city on a commuter bus one hour after my husband had left for work. We struggled through traffic until we arrived downtown, then I would disappear into a skyscraper. I had an interesting job and I was good at it. I was tough, aggressive, and always able to stay one step ahead of the competition. My husband and I met for dinner at a different restaurant every evening, then we drove home and pulled out our briefcases and worked for a few hours more.

I wanted to develop other qualities in my personality. I was tired of being hard-nosed and cynical. I wanted to get away from it all for a while. Now I spend my days as I please. One day I might swim, play tennis, or go for a long walk with the dog. Another day I might sew, paint or read. I lunch with friends and visit relatives I've barely seen in years. I love every minute of it.

When my husband arrives home in the evening dinner is all prepared. He can finish his work if he needs to, but I've noticed that since I've stopped working he brings a lot less home. We can spend our evenings together and it has really helped him to relax. I think your moods tend to rub off on each other when you are married, and I can help him more because I am so fresh and well-rested myself.

What's funny to me is that my friends think I'm crazy. I can understand their attitude because I've been in their shoes, but to me they are the ones with the distorted idea of how to live their lives. One co-worker actually told me that she thought I needed counseling. That no woman of any intelligence would stay at home, especially if she didn't have children. How can you explain it to someone? Your attitude just changes, and the things that used to seem so important to you no longer deserve your attentions. I don't want to live my life on the run. I'm young, and I want to enjoy myself and have more time to appreciate my husband and the other good things I have. And that's precisely what I am doing. I've never regretted my decision for one minute!"

It takes a great deal of spunk to thumb your nose at what is considered a normal lifestyle of motherhood and career. But, in the woman's struggle for equality what we wanted was choices. If we have real alternatives it is only fair that all women are allowed to pursue the options that seem attractive to them. They are courageous enough to risk putting aside their career in order to know themselves better, or to try a different lifestyle. If they are honest enough to give themselves time to examine their feelings about children and marriage, they should receive the respect that they deserve.

These women are happy as homemakers; and they see

themselves as no less attractive or interesting without a career, or children to hold up as proof of their accomplishments. They know almost instinctively that their true achievements will come from within.

SECTION THREE
Your New Role

In The Beginning

It isn't easy, but you make your decision and submit your resignation. Then suddenly, a whole new set of feelings emerge. You are uncertain about your future, and ask yourself "am I doing the right thing?" This ambivalance becomes even more complicated when your employer tries to change your mind, or when it's obvious that your co-workers do not understand your decision. You begin to doubt. "Is this lifestyle really so bad? Am I making a terrible mistake?" Your determination weakens. "Maybe I should stay" you think.

Your final days will be difficult, even painful. Everything will have an air of unreality to it. "Am I really doing this?" you wonder. You envision your work, and remember the things that brought you the most satisfaction. You look at your co-workers and think of the camaraderie you shared. You ponder the many hours that you've spent at your workplace, the people that have come and gone, your accomplishments and disappointments . . . and suddenly it hurts very much to have to leave. But the time comes when you must clean out your desk and say good-bye.

Staying at home will mark a major turning point in your life. There will be a tremendous period of adjustment for you to pass through both mentally and financially. No matter how happy you are about your decision there will be times when you mourn the job you left. There will be days when you feel cut off from everything that you knew so well, isolated in a role that you know little about. As with anything new and unfamiliar, you will have mixed emotions. On the one hand, you now have the tremendous freedom that you looked forward to. You can read, sleep in, and catch up on all of the things that you wanted to do when you were so busy. On the other hand, the open and empty days loom ahead. You wonder how you can possibly fill those 40-60-70 hours a week that you once devoted to your career. Like a child at Christmas, you flit from this to that, wanting to try everything at once.

There are several pitfalls to watch for in this early period. You may find that you accomplish a lot less. part of this is due to a normal drop in productivity that often accompanies major change. This is usually a temporary situation that disappears as you regain your confidence. However, three faults can appear during this time that will be difficult to eradicate later. They are:

1. When you don't have a lot to do it becomes very easy to do nothing at all.
2. You may find yourself continually distracted with trivial details that you used to ignore.
3. "Work expands so as to fill the time available for its completion." (Parkinson's law)

You will find suggestions for avoiding these traps in the chapter on "Managing Your Time".

Another part of your initial adjustment will be a feeling of disillusionment. The difficulties of living a role that provides so little esteem have become more apparent. In some ways your new life will not meet all of your expectations. In other ways it may be harder than you anticipated, especially if you thrive on structure and routine. Most of these feelings will disappear as you reach a better understanding of yourself, develop new interests, and create new activities to fill your days. As a more satisfying lifestyle begins to emerge, a second wind of energy and enthusiasm for your role will appear.

A few other women share the adjustments they faced as new homemakers:

Donna

"Due to a company policy, I had to go on maternity leave when I was eight months pregnant. The change was incredible! I went from a hectic 50 hour a week job to nearly empty days. I went from an office filled with pandemonium and a babble of voices to the silence of a ticking clock. I would stare at the calender and the days seemed to stretch ahead in a monotonous line. My life was already tedious and I felt bored and anxious. I would call the office almost every day just to listen to the excitement and commotion.

After a few weeks at home the baby's room was ready, and I found myself making friends with a neighbor I didn't even like just to pass the time. I was tired of being pregnant and wished the baby would hurry so I could return to work as quickly as possible.

Once Jason was born, so much changed! He had trouble with his formula, then he had colic, and it seemed like he was fussy or crying all the time. I began to dream about those quiet, blissful days before he was born. When it came time to return to work I didn't feel energetic enough to resume that feverish pace, and I found that I didn't like the thought of leaving Jason, especially since he was finally healthy and happy. So here I am a year later, and still a homemaker. Who would ever have believed it?"

Sharon

"When I left work I didn't have any friends who were homemakers, and my husband was out of town two days a week on business. I felt lonely, isolated and separated from everyone and everything that was familiar. It was a very hard time for me emotionally. With so much time on my hands I found myself thinking about problems in my life and marriage that I had been able to ignore until then. I also discovered how much the support and approval of other people meant to me. I felt that my husband and children took me for granted, and I craved some type of praise. But, after much painful struggle I finally learned to stand alone and find satisfaction with my own actions and approval from within."

Teresa

"At first I felt I had to justify leaving my career by being the perfect housewife. I made a big job out of housework, making my own bread, sewing the children's clothes—I never stopped working. One day my daughter said 'Mommy, I thought you weren't going to work all the time anymore.' I realized that I had left my job to spend more time with my children— not to win some sort of Suzy Homemaker award. I learned to get household things accomplished as quickly as I could—and enjoy the rest of my time! Now I might spend a whole day playing outside with the children, or a weekend sewing a new outfit for one of them, but I always keep my options open. If you accept that all things need not balance at all times, you can enjoy wonderful variety in your time at home."

Linda

"I felt isolated, withdrawn, worthless, alone, inadequate and powerless. My days, my life seemed so unimportant. I cared for my husband and children—but was that enough to give meaning to my life? I had no energy and never seemed to get anything accomplished. My husband was soon urging me to go back to work. 'You're really falling apart' he told me. I was unhappy at home, yet I didn't want to return. It was a very trying time for all of us. An accidental opportunity helped me to snap out of it. A close friend had volunteered to co-ordinate our church festival when she suddenly became ill. Since she had been doing it for years, and I had heard her discuss it so often, she insisted that I was the only person who could step into her shoes at the last minute. I hesitated because I really didn't want the responsibility, but she was so desperate that I finally agreed.

Soon my phone was ringing off the hook and I had so much going on that I didn't have time to feel sorry for myself. By the time it was all over my gloominess had completely disappeared. I felt buoyed and encouraged by my accomplishments. If I could start all over I wish that I had known that no matter who you are, or what you are doing, you must force yourself to find things that interest and stimulate your mind. You don't have to have a career, you just have to make the effort."

Jan

"Once I stopped working everything was so different. My only responsibilities were caring for the baby, straightening up the apartment, doing the laundry and making dinner. Suddenly I had all of this open-ended time on my hands. I read books I had been wanting to read for years. I visited friends and had some wonderful visits for the first time in ages. I went for walks through the park and along the river with my baby. I watched my baby grow and was fascinated to see how much she could change in just one day. In so many ways it's been an idyllic amble through life. A welcome change of pace for any new mother!"

Diane

"I lived in a vacuum at first. Somehow I thought of the real world as life at the office, while the rest of us existed in some sort of void. It took me a long time to realize that each were separate worlds functioning simultaneously and virtually oblivious to the other. I certainly never thought about the mailman or the women at the craft shop when I had a career, but now they touch my life almost every day. There are mothers at the park, the neighbors down the street, a whole new world that was just waiting for me to turn my eyes toward it. Once I did, I began to relax and form new friendships. It was the first big step toward identifying myself as a homemaker."

Carla

"After I left my career I found it hard to turn off my competitive nature. If one of my former co-workers would call and excitedly share that they had just completed a banner month, I would rack my brain trying to come up with some accomplishment of my own of equal importance. It's not really possible. I could identify with her achievements, but she couldn't with mine. At first that realization was depressing, I felt that it somehow made me less important. Then I realized that it was foolish to try and compete in such disparate areas, our values and goals are entirely different today. Now, I look to other homemakers to share satisfaction with my achievements—and when a former co-worker calls I congratulate her, and leave it at that."

What are the keys to overcoming your initial problems adjustment? Here are a few ideas:

Be an innovator: Look for ways to balance the past and future, your traditional and non-traditional needs until you are satisfied with your life.

Be resilient: Find ways to adapt to difficulties that arise, be flexible enough to refashion frustrations until you find success.

Be open to new experiences: Begin with small changes, the clothes you wear, the foods you eat, the books you read.

Nurture your curiousity by continual learning, and discover new things to fascinate your interest.

Be assured: Take steps to sustain your confidence and abilities. Create new outlets for satisfaction and reward. Take time for yourself and your needs. Develop the growth of your self-esteem.

Be committed: Do not allow disappointments and setbacks to divert you from enjoying your life. Examine your present situation and investigate the various options that you might pursue.

Be ready: To make the effort and take the steps necessary for your success. Don't delay, begin now.

Common Problems

Certain issues such as depression, loneliness, dependence, and stress can affect anyone, no matter what they do in life. But a homemaker can sometimes be more vulnerable to these problems because her role is so undefined that it is difficult for her to acknowledge them or easier to ignore them if they appear. Here is some information about these common problems:

Depression

Have you been through a major change? Suffered from prolonged stress and pressure? Held in anger? Have you felt isolated? Of course you have. All of us share these situations at one point or another in our lives, but at some stages they affect us more deeply than at others. The degree that your depression affects you can vary enormously. For one woman, it may be a series of mild feelings that appear sporadically. For another, it might be a deep, intense, continual series of symptoms. Because of the transformation of lifestyle that homemakers go through, it is not uncommon to be depressed during the initial period of adjustment. However, there are times when depression can be traced to a hormonal or chemical imbalance. If you feel depressed, visit your doctor for a checkup. There is medication to alleviate the symptoms if the problem is a physical one.

A few women share their problems with depression, however these stories reflect more severe depressive states:

Alicia

"I just wanted to be left alone. It seemed no one could understand that. My husband and my mother seemed to have a campaign going to keep me occupied. I began to withdraw further and further from everyone around me. I couldn't explain why I felt so sad and dejected, but the reason didn't matter to me any more. Then, when I was left alone, I felt isolated. I was sure that no one could relate to me or understand me. I had difficulty sleeping, and my fatigue seemed to make my feelings more pronounced. It seemed like I would never feel normal again."

Robin

"Nothing seemed worthwhile. I was gloomy, listless, and couldn't bring myself to care about anything. I stopped getting dressed, making meals and cleaning house. I barely spoke to my husband and children, or listened to their unsolicited advice. It seemed pointless to try anything or to do anything because nothing mattered. The only thing I remember feeling at that time was overwhelming guilt. 'How could I be so ungrateful for such a healthy, wonderful family?' I didn't have a *right* to be depressed. That attitude caused me to avoid the problem—you can't acknowledge something that you don't feel you have."

Paula

"Suddenly the simplest tasks seemed like an enormous undertaking. I remember attempting to tie a bow on my blouse one day, and I just couldn't concentrate enough to do it. I finally had to give up and change blouses. I couldn't make a decision. Each day I would try to think of what to make for supper and my mind would go blank. I remember the week I served chicken for three nights in a row before the family rebelled. The next night we went out to dinner, but the menu proved too much for me. I couldn't handle all of the choices. Finally, my husband had to order for me.''

If you suffer from similar problems, or any type of prolonged feelings of sadness and dejection, *take action*. The worst thing that you could do is to try and ignore the problem because depression builds on itself, and without help it can become quite severe. It doesn't matter if you believe that you have no reason to be depressed. If you are, take care of the problem. You can worry about the reasons at another time.

Once you have visited your doctor and he has determined that it is not a physical problem, then it is time to try other steps. Here are a few suggestions. Please note that most of them apply to helping milder forms of depression:

1. Find a trained, impartial counselor to talk to.
2. Discuss your feelings with your husband. He may be too close to the problem to help you resolve it, but if he is understanding and supportive it can be a tremendous help to you.
3. Social relationships provide a helpful buffer for many depressive symptoms. Force yourself to spend time with caring friends and family. It can help to lessen the seriousness of the symptoms.
4. Exercise.
5. Listen to upbeat music.
6. Visit your church or synagogue.
7. Listen to children as they laugh and play. Try to empathize with their feelings of wonder and excitement.
8. Do something for someone in need. It can take your mind off of your concerns and help you to balance

your perspective.

Loneliness

There are several kinds of loneliness a homemaker can suffer from. There is the inevitable feeling of responsibility. That even with a supportive husband and good friends you are entirely on your own. You may be used to operating in a team environment, now you must motivate yourself and make sure that the work is done. You'll find an obvious lack of sympathetic companionship because most people work outside of the home. Those few homemakers that you are acquainted with may be of some help, but it won't be easy co-ordinating your children's schedules for regular get togethers. There is also the feeling that most of the people that you are close to, your husband, former co-workers, and friends who work can no longer understand you or relate to your problems because your concerns are now so different. Lastly, there is the longing you feel for your absent former self. "What happened to the outgoing career woman who had acquired respect, was always well-groomed, and had so many social exchanges each day?" One woman describes her feelings of loneliness:

Barb

"I was more concerned about preserving my privacy after I first left my career. I had this mental picture of neighbors that continually rang my doorbell to 'borrow' something as an excuse to chat. I was afraid that my kitchen would be filled every morning with gossiping women drinking my coffee while their children whined and tumbled about. I would never have time for myself or get anything done. Worse yet, I would become just like they were. Boy, was I in for a surprise!

There are very few people left in my neighborhood after nine a.m. I know of three other stay-at-home mothers. They are friendly enough and we have exchanged a few visits, but they are busy and preoccupied with their own lives and interests. I find myself trying to think of something to 'borrow' as an excuse for a chat.

The baby sleeps while I eat my lunch and listen to a radio talk show. I linger over my coffee wishing my kitchen was filled with other women, no matter what they talked about. I feel so remote, secluded from the outside world. I find myself calling working friends as soon as they get in the door. I wish I had known and prepared for this. I had no idea what it would be like. At least I know that once the baby is older I will be able to get out and do more. But right now, it's very, very, hard."

Loneliness can bring on other unhappy feelings such as insecurity, self-doubt, and anxiety. The pain that you feel may make you angry—at yourself, loved ones, or at everyone else around you. You may begin to demand that others fill your needs by providing continual companionship or support. You may be shocked by your own behavior.

The best way to eliminate loneliness is to take action. If you are temporarily stuck at home, use that time to set goals and consider new interests. There are several chapters in this book that can help. Loneliness, like depression, can compound itself if you don't find ways to relieve it.

Dependence

It is somewhat ironic that we self-sufficient career women often fear dependence the most. We are afraid that somehow as our new role transforms us we will begin to rely on our husbands and children too heavily for support or for our identity. These misgivings are well-founded, since over-dependence was one of the primary problems for home-makers in previous generations. That doesn't mean that it is inevitable that you become overly dependent. By keeping one eye on it as a potential problem, you can continue to maintain the identity and self-sufficiency that you enjoyed when you were working. You will find other discussions of dependence in different parts of this book, but let's touch on the main points here:

1. Find ways to bolster your self-confidence on your own. Don't rely on others to do it for you.
2. Continue your quest for personal growth and self-knowledge. As you firmly entrench your identity it will be more difficult to transfer it somewhere else.
3. Have realistic expectations towards yourself and others.

Stress

I bet you couldn't wait to leave the pressures and intolerable strains of your job. You were ready to take stress, and headaches and anxiety and cast it to the winds. Not so fast. Your life will be different and your worries and concerns will change. But you still can have stress in your life.

Stress comes from within, the way that you think. In affect, you view life in stressful ways. It is a strain on your system, a result of excessive demands that you have made on your inner resources. Too much stress can provoke emotions such as depression and powerlessness; and physiological symptoms such as headaches, insomnia, chest pains, and heart palpitations. The wearing affects of continued stress may cause hypertension, asthma, ulcers, and frequent colds.

Stress can affect everything in your life, from your ability to communicate to your ability to get things done. It can affect your tolerance for other people, your willingness to resolve differences, and your sexual desire. Too often, one's response to stress results in excessive dependence on alcohol and drugs.

What causes stress? To much pressure on your vulnerable points. Stress can be a result of too much worry, anxiety, and unreasonable standards. Change is a big prelude to stress. As a new homemaker you are changing your routines, habits, rythms, diet and relationships, which is more than enough to strain any system.

We have heard about stress-prone 'Type A' personalities, and housewives are not immune to this syndrome. They can be just as hard-driven, aggressive, and hectic as their counterparts in the outside workforce. In a recent speech before the American Psychological Association, B. Kent Houston said "Housewives with driven personalities feel the same stress, fear, and dissatisfaction as career men and women with Type A personalities according to a recent study . . . He administered tests to housewives and found that compared with easygoing housewives, the Type A homemakers found housework more taxing, reported less satisfaction in their marriages, and felt more stress and tension . . . " (Post Tribune 8/85)

What do you find stressful? Make a list of incidents that have caused feelings of stress in the past. Are these problems usually brought on by your own actions? By other people? By situations? Is there anything that you can change? Because stress comes from within we each respond to it differently and we must deal with it in our own way. Here are some suggestions for easing or eliminating stress.

1. Consider how you currently respond to stressful situations. Do you hide from the problem? Feel sorry for yourself? Simmer? Explode? Take the time to analyze your responses and look for a more effective way to handle the pressure.
2. Ask yourself "Who's problem is it?" If it is something beyond your control, or in the past, stop allowing it to affect your present. If you ask yourself "How important is it?" you may decide that it really isn't worth the affect it is having on your life.
3. Because stress is a result of the way that you view things, practice changing your attitude toward matters that upset you.
4. If you can, eliminate stress causing factors from your life. If that is not possible, try to de-sensitize

your responses to them.

5. Learn to create more balance in your life. Master current problems before you take on new challenges.
6. Set limits on your expectations. You can't have it all or do it all every time. Lowering your expectations is not the same thing as lowering your standards.
7. Look for outside support. Talk to your husband or a friend about your frustrations. They may provide new insights for you to consider.
8. Don't box yourself into a corner, or allow yourself to believe that your problem is insurmountable. Your options may be limited, but there is always at least one to consider.
9. Force yourself to slow your pace. Remember, unless it's a matter of life and death, nothing can be as urgent as you are telling yourself it is. Learn to relax.
10. Develop your sense of humor. Romain Gary once said "Humor is an affirmation of dignity, a declaration of man's superiority to all that befalls him." If you can find humor in situations that trouble you, they won't seem as bad as you had thought.
11. Distance yourself from the problem by diverting your attention to other interests.
12. Understand that you will not have instant success in eliminating stress. Make slow, steady progress towards overcoming your problems.

Living It

Just as with any other new job, you may have initial feelings of trepidation about your life at home. All possibilities lie before you. The territory is slightly familiar, but you are unsure of its parameters. You may rush in, or take it slow and easy as you define your place in this new sphere. You soon discover that the field is wide open, and there is no set pattern that you must follow. A homemaker operates on instinct, experience, and innovation. Yet, in practical terms there is one concern that all new homemakers have. How will you spend your time? Although there are many answers for that question, there is one portion of our lives that we all have in common—caring for the home.

To be contented at home you must destroy any feeling you may have that housework is now your prime occupation. You are not married to a house, and caring for it needn't be an all-consuming task, nor a justification for leaving your career. Of course you must do what is necessary, but you needn't do any more than that. It is most likely that you lowered your standards of housekeeping while you were working at your paying career. While you will probably want to upgrade your criterion in some areas, you needn't compete for some type of seal of approval for a sparkling home. In any event, there isn't one. Your home should be what you, your husband, and your children can live in most comfortably.

Housework is a most difficult job. It is repetitive. Everything that you clean must be cleaned again, sometimes as soon as you finished it the first time. In fact, the cleaner your house is, the more noticeable the first signs of disarray. It is frustrating. Your family will seldom notice a spotless home, but will be quick to point out a dirty one. It is thankless. You spend hours planning, preparing, and shopping for meals that are consumed in a manner of minutes. In fact, the better the food tastes, the faster it will disappear.

There is nothing to show for your achievements. No rewards, no promotions, honors or pay raises. For a hard-working, competitive, aggressive woman, this lack of acknowledgment may impel her to try harder for some type of recognition. This will only make the task more difficult than ever.

In addition, it is easy to become possessive of something that exhausts so much of your time. The home becomes your territory, and you defend your hard work with vigor. If you vacuum and the children bring out their toys (and it's always the ones with a million detachable parts) you insist that they put them away. "I just swept in here!" you cry. If you've cleared the clutter and shined and polished the living room, the first stray article is immediately banished. "I just cleaned this room!" you say. You would be better off accepting that when you have children, this outlook is doomed. If you wish to have cleanliness as proof of your efforts, you will find yourself overcome and defeated at every turn. Your best bet is to set a goal, accomplish it, and leave it at that. You vacuumed the carpet. It is now cleaner than it was before, and no matter what you do it is going to get dirty again. At some point, you will have to vacuum again. The time and energy that you expend trying to delay the next vacuuming will probably cost you more in irritation and anxiety than it would to repeat the task.

Getting Help

Unless your children are older they will only provide minimal assistance towards home upkeep. In fact, the effort you must put out to get them to complete their tasks may not seem worth the bother. It is. You are making them appreciate the necessity and energy it takes to care for a home, and they'll realize it in about twenty years. In the mean time, you can hope that enough of it will stick so that they can help you more when they are older.

That leaves only one other responsible adult in your household that may provide assistance. Your husband. There is no point in talking about the ones who like housework, who voluntarily share it equally with their wives who are homemakers. They are rare and valued commodities, and chances are no wife would admit that she had one for fear of him being kidnapped in the night. The rest of us have husbands who hate housework, and rejoiced when we left our jobs because they felt that excused them from further duties. Even when you do convince them to help, they have standard ways to wiggle out of requests, such as:

A. You didn't tell me.
B. You would do it better.
C. Show me again.
D. You wouldn't like the way that I would do it.
E. All of the above.

Another problem is that men seldom have any appreciation for the things that you do. They assume that it takes little time, skill, or ability to maintain a home, and base their presumption on the two hours, one day, or one weekend that they filled in for you. They calmly point to those short term successes, conveniently forgetting that you had everything prepared for them, all instructions neatly written out, and that the house looked like a bomb had been dropped in it when you arrived home. Once, when I was in the hospital for a week, my husband proudly assured me how easily he was keeping everything in smooth running order. He was even doing the laundry. It was wonderful to know that I could go home and recuperate without worrying about the mounting household tasks. When I arrived home, I had to walk through the laundry room on the way in. There I discovered an entire weeks worth of clothes nicely washed and dried—and piled into a mountain of unfolded clothes.

What About Outside Help?

Most of us never seriously consider hiring someone else to do our housework. It seems too much of an extravagance, a luxury out of our reach when we are still trying to adjust to one salary. Although it is true that a full-time live-in maid would cost more than most of us could afford, there are other alternatives if you look for them.

Frankly, it's a matter of priorities. You may not hesitate to pay someone to do your hair, but you balk at the idea of paying someone to wash your windows. If you tried, you might be able to juggle the cost of extra help to hire a high school or college student. It might be for a temporary situation such as the heavy cleaning in Spring or Fall or around the holidays. Or there may be one household chore that you absolutely hate to do that really makes housework a drudgery for you. For example, a friend of mine hates to do floors. She pays a 14 year-old neighbor girl $15 a week to vacuum and mop all of her floors. My friend feels wonderful when she sees the work done without her having to lift a finger. The girl is thrilled to have a steady income, since she is too young to be hired anywhere else.

If there is nothing left in the weekly budget for even the slightest assistance, consider trading jobs with someone else. Perhaps you hate to dust, but don't mind doing windows. If you know someone who doesn't mind dusting but hates windows—switch! Enterprising women have traded meal making, wall papering, yard work, whatever pleased or displeased them. By eliminating chores that you truly dislike, housework will seem a little less dreary.

There are benefits to cleaning. For one thing, it is good exercise. The American Heart Association rates it with walking 3 miles per hour or bicycling 5 miles per hour for conditioning and increased oxygen intake (Reader's Digest 12/84). The physical work can provide an outlet for your pent up frustrations. It can also give you satisfaction for a job well done.

What you must bear in mind, is that an immaculate home is never as important as the people who live in it. If you do what you must as a gift to those who live there, it might make the difference between your thinking of it as drudgery or fun. A few other women share their feelings about housework:

Pat

"I finally convinced my husband to help me more around the house. With three small children it was impossible to get everything done. But I soon gave up. Every task he did, no matter how simple it seemed, was preceded and superceded by questions. Take for example—cooking potatoes. It's something that you seldom even think about, you just do it—right? Here are the questions I had to answer:

How many potatoes do we need?
What do I peel them with?
Where do I put the peels?
What do I do about these marks (eyes)?
How should I cut the potatoes?
What pot should I use?
Is this the right one?
How much water do I put in it?
Hot or cold?
Is this the right amount?
Do I boil the water before I put the potatoes in?
How high should the gas be?
Should I use a lid?
How do I know when they're done?
Why are they boiling over?

At first I thought 'well once he learns I won't have to answer all of these questions.' After I discovered that a man who can recall all of the details necessary to design a home cannot remember how to do any task without being talked through it at least five times. I gave up.''

Marie

"I don't mind housework. When I was working I had to stay mentally sharp every minute, there was little time to relax. By evening I was too drained or tired to ponder anything but sleep. Now, when I am cleaning I can shift gears and let my mind wander. I can evaluate problems while I sort the laundry, work through solutions while I dust, and let my imagination run wild while I vacuum. I play music to suit my mood while I work, and I feel refreshed and revitalized when I'm done. Then there are days when I'm angry and housework is an outlet for my frustrations. I can scrub away hurts as I do the floors, and let off steam as I vacuum. When I'm done I'm not tired and drained, but soothed and invigorated.''

Sue

''When I worked, I did what housework I could fit in on weekends and let the rest go. It didn't bother me if someone dropped in and the house was cluttered . . . 'after all I had more important things to do'. Once I stayed home, I saw housework as my job, and the only measure there was of my performance. I was almost obsessed with making everything perfect, I found myself caught up in the most trivial details. Once I spent an entire day taking a spot out of the carpet. I reached the point where I hated cleaning, but I felt that I was obliged to keep at it as 'my part of the bargain'.

One beautiful weekend my husband suggested that we get away to the country. I had had a cold all week and the house was a mess. 'I can't go' I told him. 'I didn't get the house cleaned.' 'So what'' he said. 'Clean it next week.' 'But I wouldn't be able to enjoy myself knowing that I didn't do my job' I answered. He couldn't believe it. 'That's the most ridiculous thing I've ever heard' he said. 'Do you realize how dull you have become? You need to get out more.' That really hurt. 'But I'm trying to keep the house nice for you' I said. 'Me?' his voice got louder. 'I don't care about having a spotless house, I never have. You created the problem yourself. Haven't I been telling you to get out more and find other things to do?' 'I know' I answered, 'but I never have time'. He grabbed my arm. 'You're making time now' he said, 'we'll pick up what we need on the way.'

Of course it was an enjoyable outing, and I hadn't realized how locked in my life had become until I got away from it for a while. I'm out of that phase now, and believe me I've found plenty of other things to do with my time!''

Joan

''Everyone in my family loved the holiday meals at our house, except for me. After a week of scrubbing, polishing, vacuuming, dusting, and running to the grocery store seven times in three days, the relatives would descend upon our home. They would talk and chatter, and seldom offer to help. I would spend the entire meal jumping up and down getting items that were forgotten or requested at the last minute. Once everyone left, it would take a few days to get the house back in order.

One year I decided—no more. I was fed up with spending my holidays tired, irritable, and angry. I told the entire family that if they wanted to celebrate Christmas at our house (we have the most room) I wanted help. If at least one person from each family didn't provide some assistance, they wouldn't be welcome. I made an exception for my 80 year old grandmother, but she insisted on helping too! A few days before Christmas I had a housecleaning party. I assigned everyone tasks, showed them where everything was, and set my grandmother to polishing the silver. Then I took my list and went shopping. I didn't have as much to buy because each family was going to bring a dish. It worked out wonderfully. I really enjoyed the holiday. Now I understand that my true role was not to be a servant, it was to be a co-ordinator.''

Friends

With the housework out of the way, our husbands and friends at work, and our children to young for conversation, most homemakers crave adult companionship. Such social contact is important to everyone, and the support of someone who can identify with your feelings can be a major boost to making your transition an easier one. Friendships are important. Studies by the California Department of Health (Vogue 4/85) show that good friends help us to avoid serious emotional problems because they provide a buffer of approval. "People who cut themselves off from others have 2-3 times the risk of an early death . . . (and) a better chance of getting cancer . . . "

Homemakers have a special appreciation of friendship because they are more prone to loneliness. However, it is not always easy to create new relationships outside the home. It may be that you left many friends behind at your job, but unless you socialized with them outside of work, the chances are that these relationships will eventually fade away. In the mean time, you want to create new contacts that can relate to your new lifestyle. How many friends do you have now? One way to discover this is to write your name at the top of a sheet of paper. Then list all of the people that you are closest to, that you can count on the most. Does the number of people that you can rely on surprise you? Then add the names of people that you feel comfortable with, no matter how long it has been since you have seen them. Are there people that you deeply care for that you have been neglecting? Now is the time to renew those friendships that can mean so much to you.

We all need several different types of friends. You need those that you can count on in a crisis. You need pals that you can enjoy activities with. You need someone to share the latest advances of your children. Most importantly, you need friends who will motivate and uplift you. It isn't easy to make new acquaintances, and turn them into deeper relationships. If you have young children it may not be easy to get out. You can meet other women through your own activities, or through those designed for children. Parks, schools, pools, craft fairs, exercise classes, library reading hours, and local and church activities are all sources for potential acquaintances. Children are a great ice-breaker, as are common interests. Everyone that you meet won't be suited to be an intimate friend, but as you expand the list of people that you know you will have a better chance of making real friendships.

Communication
What will you talk about with the new friends that you meet, or with the old co-workers that you run into? After years of discussing your job, you may find it difficult to find interesting topics in your daily life. Yet, the key to good conversation is not the topic that you discuss, but how it is handled. People like to talk about themselves, and they enjoy speaking with people who make them feel good about themselves. That doesn't mean that you need to bombard them with flattery, but it helps to start the conversation by getting them to talk about things that they feel comfortable with. This is easiest if you talk about feelings and ideas instead of facts. In other words, instead of asking someone "Why did you move to this area?" which will probably receive a short response, ask "How do you feel about living in this area?"

Finding Happiness
Not all homemakers are satisfied with their new lifestyle. Two women share their feelings:

Jenny
"I liked my job. It was wonderful to start a project, see it through to the finish, and at times be rewarded for it. At home it is so different. Cleaning our apartment doesn't take long, but it seems like I do it over and over again. I miss the people that I worked with, the daily contact, the approval, the stimulation they provided. I love being with my baby, but sometimes I feel that the walls are closing in."

Jean
"I want it all. I want to be an executive and carry a

briefcase and wear nice clothes and use my brain for more than sorting laundry. Yet, I want to be here with my twins to hear every cute word and see every first move. I'm afraid to talk to other working women because I am sure that I am too boring. I can't help it! If someone asks me what I do I say 'I'm just a housewife' because that is all that I feel I am."

How can you find happiness at home? Here are a few ideas:

Be innovative. Use your creativity to pursue new or existing interests. If your old interests don't suit your life any more, find new ones. You can function productively without someone else setting your goals and deadlines for you if you make the effort.

Find control. Happy people all share the feeling that they have some control in their lives. Take steps by examining your situation and finding ways that you can regain this feeling. Don't give up until you are satisfied.

Look for support. Talk to your husband, family, or friends. Don't worry about boring them, that is what friends are for.

Knock down barriers. Don't fool yourself by believing that there is no time for your own goals and interests, or that there are no activities that you want to pursue. You need other interests, you deserve other interests, you must have other interests in your life.

Never stop growing. Sometimes it is easier to follow someone else's script for your life than trying to write your own. Yet, to stay independent you must learn, read, ask, examine, study, struggle and expand yourself continually. You must learn and understand your needs before you can have fulfillment.

Happiness is intangible. You can't buy it, see it, or inherit it, you have to create it by living every hour of your day in pursuit of it. Only then, will you capture momentary experiences that will delight, gratify and please you—and make it all worthwhile.

Your New Baby

The majority of women who become homemakers decide to leave their jobs after the birth of their first child. Many plan to resume their careers after returning from maternity leave, but change their minds at some point. Others prefer to delay their return to the workforce until a later date. Whatever the case, most women feel trapped in a tremendous tug-of-war when making this decision.

On the one hand, there is an enormous pull towards staying at home with your baby. How can you leave such a tiny, helpless little creature who was so recently a part of you? You and your baby have shared every moment of his life until now, and it isn't easy to break that bond. Opposing your family life are the realities of working. You don't relish the thought of getting up early, coming home late, and trying to enjoy motherhood while you are distracted by job pressures. But, you still have a career. You may have had to go to great lengths to convince your boss that being a mother would not affect your future work, and you are not sure if you want to give up the excitement, challenge and salary that you have become so accustomed to. You are torn by the same feelings that all women who consider leaving the workforce have, but your decision is complicated by this overwhelming change in your life—the baby.

Your body has gone through a physical upheaval that will take months, even years, to fully recover from. Your emotions, your identity, your marriage and your home life will never be the same. You need time to acclimate yourself to these many adjustments, and this reality is born out by years of tradition. In fact, most societies have always encouraged mothers to draw away from the demands of daily life for some period after giving birth. The only exception to this period of isolation has been among the very poor. Those women always had to get up at once and return to the fields or the stove. Today, most women are expected to resume their careers as quickly as possible, and because of this many are not giving themselves enough time at home. According to Dr. T. Berry Brazelton (Family Circle 9/24/85):

Research suggests that stages of development in the mother-infant relationship during the first four months are critical for baby and mother. During this period you are learning about yourself as nurturer and the baby as a person. You are developing a communication system with your baby: you learn to read each other's signals through body language, smiles, eye contact and ''talk'' (you speak reassuringly; baby turns to look at you; you learn to coax your baby to smile) . . . Unless a woman can be with her baby during this special bonding period, she may never feel completely successful in caring for him. In infant-parent relationships where this interaction wasn't successfully completed, we've seen infants fail to thrive—socially, mentally and even physically.

You have a special relationship with your child, and you may even feel that you have an instinct or sixth sense that warns you of your child's needs. Another person can provide clean diapers, bottles and some care, but no one is as intensely aware of what is best for your child as you are. Yet, the decision to try full-time motherhood is sometimes a very difficult one because there is never the assurance that your decision will be the best for you and your family. Your career is familiar to you and it is an area of your life where you have already proven that you can succeed and maintain control. It is very hard to willingly walk away from that and take on the insecurities of homemaking and parenthood. In addition, caring for a child calls for very different qualities of attitude and behavior than a successful job does. In your work it is necessary to be aggressive, assertive, competitive, goal-oriented and to follow orders. At home with a child you must be tender, caring, giving, nurturing, self-sacrificing and on your own.

A few other women share problems they encountered while making the transition, and explain how they solved them:

Gail

"I returned to work six weeks after Jennifer was born and I felt like I was being torn to pieces every day. I would get ready for work in the morning and end up redoing my makeup because I couldn't stop crying. I didn't want to leave my soft, cuddly, sweet-smelling baby daughter and battle traffic to the office, where I had to transform myself into a hard-nosed executive. Inevitably, Jen would be crying when I left, and although I knew she was too young to understand that I was leaving, each little cry that I would hear as I walked down the steps would be like a knife turning inside me. At work I would fall into my routine, but she was never far from my mind. I would catch myself thinking of her during tough negotiations and marveling at the contrast between that softness and the harsh language that I was hearing. After a month I decided that although I liked my career, it wasn't what I wanted at this point in my life. I talked it over with my husband and although he was less than enthusiastic he finally agreed that it would be the best move for all of us. I'm not sure how long I will stay home, one year—three years—six years, but I am sure that I won't leave again until Jennifer and I can part comfortably."

Karen

"I decided not to return to work after Melissa was

born. My job took an enormous amount of effort and concentration, and I knew that I would have to work twice as hard to prove to my boss that having a baby hadn't changed me. Although my career had always been a big part of my life, I was now a completely different person . . . I was a mother. I wanted to be able to focus all of my attention on my daughter, as well as my time and my energy. I didn't want to miss one part of the experience. I knew I couldn't handle both my family and my career without driving myself to distraction, so I chose to concentrate my attention to this part of my life for now.''

Christine

"I welcomed the chance to stay home after Daniel was born. I was tired of working. The long hours and the political infighting that daily took place in our department was very draining. The thought of peace, quiet and an adorable baby was all that I was interested in, I could set my own pace, create my own routine, and have only myself, my husband and baby to worry about. Of course the reality of staying home with a newborn wasn't quite what I had hoped it would be, but it was still a welcome change.''

Michele

To do my job well requires about fifty hours a week, and to do it and get ahead requires about seventy hours of work every week. I was organized, willing to put in my time, and I never doubted that I could handle a job and a baby too. But there's a huge difference between working at a job where you can get up and leave when you've had enough, and a job that never ends. A child is a twenty-four hour a day responsibility, and just knowing that can be draining on your system. You can hire a sitter, but if they don't show up you are left to handle the problem. You can arrange to place your child in a daycare center, but if the child is sick, you must make sure that he is properly taken care of. It is a big adjustment to realize that you can't be number one anymore; and an overwhelming feeling when you realize that you are a mother 24 hours a day for life.''

Denise

''One day the sitter canceled at the last minute and I couldn't find a back-up. There was a report that had to be completed that day, and my husband was out of town. I didn't feel that I had a choice in the matter, so I packed Samantha's things and took her with me. I had heard stories of women who have their children brought to the office to breast feed, or who have taken them to work when necessary. It hadn't yet happened in our office, but (since we have no clients who actually enter our department) I didn't anticipate any tremendous problems . . . especially since my boss had three all children of his own.

I went directly to his office and explained the situation. I suggested that I would take my work to a back office and remain there with the door shut, and would make every effort not to disrupt the office routine. 'No, get her out of here!' he said. I reminded him of the report that absolutely had to be completed and sent to our home office that day. 'Look' he said. 'You wanted to be a mother, so be one. Take your baby home and take care of her. I'll have John finish your report.'

I sat there stunned. I honestly couldn't move. This was the same man who had continually praised my work; given me this project because he insisted that only I could do it right, and even had told me fond stories of his children's births while I was pregnant. Now he was talking to me as if I were an errant five-year old. It dawned on me then that I had put myself in an awkward predicament. Knowing my boss as well as I did, I could just hear him when I was up for my next promotion—or if I tried to use him as a reference to find a new job: 'She was fine until she had a baby, then I don't know—she lost her touch. She even brought the baby to work!'

I had heard rumors that this man loved to pirate ideas from his employees, but so far in the year we had worked together he was always careful to give me credit for everything I did. The project I had just completed was one of the largest we'd ever been asked to do—and suddenly it hit me—he had been looking for a way to get me out of here so that he could put his own name on my report. He encouraged me to stay on maternity leave as long as I liked, and perhaps he had hoped that I wouldn't return to work at all. Now, he had a way. If I wasn't here to complete the report, he could easily portray my role as a secondary one.

'I'm sorry for the misunderstanding' I told him. 'I do have a few last minute notes in my head that I'd like to add, then I'll leave.' I knew that I had guessed right when I saw the smug look on his face. I went to my office and quickly made a few changes, a number here, a word there; enough to make the work inaccurate. Then I pulled the personal items from my desk, picked up the still-sleeping Samantha and left. That afternoon I typed my resignation and had it sent by messenger. It was a very sudden move on my part, and neither I or my husband were prepared for the instant change. Yet, I'm really glad now that it turned out the way it did because I enjoy staying home a great deal more than I would ever have thought. It also gives me time to consider different career options for when I return to work. My old boss? They demoted him after he turned in such a lousy report!"

Vicky

"I didn't plan to stay at home, yet once the baby was

born the days seemed to fly by. I was so immersed in him and our new lives that I completely lost track of time. I had been home seven weeks when my supervisor's secretary called. 'I just wanted to verify that you'll be returning to work next week as scheduled' she said. I hadn't given work more than a vague thought and I couldn't imagine going back there in a week. 'Let me call you back' I told her. I hung up the phone and looked around me. Motherhood had been more tiring than I had imagined. There had been days when I was lonely, bored and depressed, but since I had always considered my hiatus a temporary one those feelings never became an overwhelming problem. I had never even considered staying home full-time. I couldn't imagine not going back to the career that I had spent so many years building.

But how could I leave my baby when he's growing so fast? When he hears my voice he smiles. When I come into the room he kicks with pleasure. There are times when I'm talking to him that he almost seems to be trying to answer me. Just last week he found his hands and it's fascinating to watch him open his fingers then pull at them and stare and stare. It's so incredible to watch his wonder and amazement as he begins to discover the world around him. I know that this is just the beginning too. There are so many things waiting up ahead, how could I miss any of it?

I called my husband at work. 'They want me back on the job next week' I told him. 'I know' he answered. 'I've been looking forward to your getting a full paycheck again.' I started crying. 'I don't want to leave my baby!' I said. 'Stop being so dramatic' he said impatiently. 'You like working, and you always said that you would go insane if you had to stay home all day. This is just a phase you're going through.' I wondered if he was right, if I was having some type of hormonal reaction that would fade in time. 'It's like when you take a vacation' he continued. 'The first day back is always the hardest, but once you fall into your old routine it doesn't seem so bad after all.' I promised to think about it some more.

Deep down I didn't feel ready to resume my career. I knew that if I didn't go back next week I would be expected to resign. To leave a twelve-year job seemed so final—and if I did stay at home—what would I do all day? I need time for me. I need other people to talk to. I need to have challenges and excitement—and I didn't think I could find it outside the workforce. Then there was my salary. Was it possible for us to get by without it? I brought out the calculator and did some fast figuring. We could do it, but it would be an incredibly tight squeeze. It would mean cutting back on *everything*: the way we ate (no more steaks), the way we lived (no more big vacations), and even the way we dressed— would it be worth it? I truly felt it was. I had always followed my instincts, and they told me that I needed more time at home.

I called my husband back. This time I was more business-like. I rattled off the pros and cons, cut short his arguments, then explained the new budget. He sighed. 'Do you know how hard it's going to be to live on my salary?' he asked. 'You have never had to live on a tight budget before—what makes you think you could do it?' 'If it doesn't work, I can always find another job' I told him. 'I think you are going to be very unhappy at home full-time' he said but do what you want to do.''

I called my boss. 'I'm submitting my resignation' I told him. He wasn't happy either. 'You're not the type of woman to stay at home' he told me. 'I think you are going to regret it. You know, my wife had the same feelings, but she returned to her job and she loves it.' I felt the doubts creeping back, but I stuck to my decision. No one approved of it, but I was happy. Suddenly I felt incredibly free—like I'd just been given an extra vacation.''

Adjusting To A New Baby

Your baby will bring out feelings and emotions that you never knew you had. For some women there's an immediate rush of motherly feeling, for others it is a slow and gradual process. You may feel distant from the baby at first, or disappointed that your new life isn't exactly as you expected it to be. Some disappointment is almost inevitable. You spent nine months building up anticipation of the baby, but there is almost always an emotional letdown after such a major event. No matter how many books you read or people you talk to, you will discover that advice may help, but living is the only way to gain experience.

Suddenly, a demanding stranger has entered your life, and every other aspect of your being seems to spin out of control. Your baby cries and you become over-anxious and frustrated. Your days fly by and you often forget to start dinner. Your husband seems like a passing stranger. You may be afraid to accept anyone's help in caring for the child because you feel that you must provide everything for the baby as you did throughout the pregnancy. Yet, it will never be possible to fulfill all of your child's needs. There will be times when you won't be able to comfort him, and times when he will make you unhappy—even angry at his behavior. You must understand and accept the fact that this is a part of the adjustment to motherhood, if you don't you will be miserable. The truth is, there are so many different emotions involved here that it's almost impossible for you to describe how you really feel. Clearer insight usually begins to dawn after five or six months. A few other women share how they felt as new mothers:

Brenda

"I knew motherhood wasn't always easy, but nothing prepared me for how difficult it could be. There were days when she seemed so precious and adorable one minute, and a tiring source of drudgery the next. There were times when I would sit and watch her sleep and think 'she's the most beautiful thing in the world'. There were other times that I'd see her stir, and her face would scrunch up like she was going to cry—and I'd think 'please God no, not again'. There were times when I was so tired I was afraid that I would drop her, and times when I wanted to sit and hold her forever. Jim had to work such long hours back then that he wasn't able to be of much help. I felt lonely and isolated, yet when I did talk with anyone else I would spend the entire time talking about the baby!"

Diane

"I didn't feel like a mother at all. I felt a strange detachment for this baby who seemed nice enough, but hardly connected with me. My lack of feeling scared me. I would listen to other women gush and carry on about their babies and I would think 'what's wrong with me?' I felt so guilty, but I didn't know what I could do about it. I didn't want to mention it to anyone else because I was sure they would think I was a horrible person. Luckily, my cousin guessed what was happening. One day she came for a visit and while I was making coffee she said: 'You know when Amanda was born I felt absolutely nothing. I kept waiting for this rush of motherly love, and it just wasn't there. I would think well maybe when I feed her it will come. It didn't. I hoped that it might appear when I brought her home, or when I gave her a bath. But nothing happened. Actually, I was so nervous when I gave her a bath I wouldn't have noticed the feeling if it walked in and hit me over the head'. I smiled through my tears. She looked at me. 'Women are afraid to talk about this lack of feeling, but it happens more often than you would suspect. I never could tell anyone until I joined a mother's support group. They helped me to get through it—and to understand that I wasn't alone. I think groups like that are just as important as childbirth classes, because you need to talk about your feelings to people who aren't emotionally involved.' 'So what did you do?' I asked. I knew how attached she was to two-year old Amanda. 'I stopped trying' she said. 'You can't make yourself feel like a mother, it just has to happen. Sometimes a baby has to grow on you, just like any other new person in your life'.

I felt so relieved! Just knowing that I wasn't alone, or somehow crippled emotionally was so wonderful. It helped me to relax around my baby and enjoy him more. Of course, my cousin was right. As time passed I felt all of the caring, loving feelings that I had dreamed about when I was pregnant.''

Alison

"When they wheeled me into the delivery room I thought 'this is it, now you are going to be a mother.' Those three words 'this is it' ran clickety-clack through my mind every day for the next few weeks. Once you become a mother, it's for life. There's no turning back, no changing your mind. You can't resign. Of course I understood the depth of commitment that parenthood takes before I became pregnant. But knowing it and living it are entirely different. So much had changed in such a short time. I missed the me who could do what she wanted whenever she pleased. One day I caught myself getting ready to go out to the car and run to the store. For a brief moment, I had completely forgotten the sleeping baby in the next room! When I realized what I'd almost done, I felt guilty—and more trapped than ever.

Ironically, my first outing didn't work out very well. When Matt was two-weeks old my mother came over and insisted that I get out for a few hours. I hopped in my car and drove to a nearby shopping mall. I felt such a wonderful sense of freedom, I couldn't believe that I could finally do something for myself. Yet, I also couldn't stop thinking about Matt. 'What was he doing now? Was he crying?' I realized I was being ridiculous, but I couldn't get him out of my mind. I was home after an hour—I couldn't stay away any longer. It's like what they used to say about husbands: I couldn't live with my baby, but I couldn't live without him either."

Mary

"There's no way you can prepare for the powerful attachment that you feel for your baby. I felt so intensely involved in everything—each cough, each little move, every cry. I was so afraid that something would happen to her that I would check her every half hour when she was sleeping to make sure that everything was okay. It's an attachment that's so hard to describe. I still felt as if she were a part of me, as she had been for nine whole months. I couldn't stop thinking about her, talking about her or reading baby books. It was an incredible time."

Other Feelings You May Have

There are several other problems you may face as a new mother. Here are a few:

I'm a slave. This incredibly demanding creature requires continual care and supervision. Even when you are not physically handling him you are doing his laundry, washing his bottles, etc. You give, give and give, and what do you receive in return? Crying, messy diapers, and wake-up calls throughout the night. It is not until the baby grows older and begins to respond to your attentions that you feel some reward for your efforts. In the mean time, brace yourself because it's going to be a mostly one-sided deal for quite a few years to come.

I'm jealous! During your pregnancy all of the attention was focused on you. Strangers would stop and ask you 'When are you due?' 'Are you hoping for a boy or a girl?' Often they would go on to share some childbirth experience of their own. Your husband and co-workers were extremely conscious and often overly solicitous of your condition. After the baby is born, the attention you received is gone. People come over to see the baby. Your husband comes home and asks about the baby. Your house seems invaded by baby things everywhere you turn. Who wouldn't feel a little bit jealous? That is why contact with other mothers is so helpful, they are going through the same thing.

I feel so guilty. There are times when your baby makes you angry. You may wish momentarily that you weren't a mother. You know that there were days when you didn't change his diaper as fast as you should have, or when you were too tired to give him a bath. You are not perfect. No mother is. Just repeat over and over "I'm doing the best I can". That is all your baby needs.

I am not sure of who I am anymore. You are going through an enormous change. You are still the young girl who suffered through her first date and the young woman who married your husband. Now you have a triple identity— yourself, someone's wife, and someone's mom. Just as it took time to find yourself and to adjust to marriage, it will take more time before you feel comfortable being a mother. You will need to find answers for the questions that every new mother faces, such as: "How will the baby affect my life?", "My marriage?", and "Will I ever have time to be myself again?" There is a good reason for feeling that your whole life is in a state of flux. It is. You are passing through another period of growth and development and creating a new sense of self. You may discover that as you struggle with this new identity you may have to re-hash long-buried conflicts within yourself. Often problems and disappointments from childhood come back to disturb you at this time. Don't fight this struggle because it is all part of the inevitable growth process that will help you to mature in your new role.

I'm not sure of what I'm doing. Who doesn't secretly believe that mothers automatically know how to care for their children? But it is not automatic. It takes time to get to know your baby's personality and his different cries. You can't know right away if he likes to be walked or rocked when he's restless. Just as your attitudes and theories about childraising w ill change as you adapt them to this child's personality, your knowledge of what your baby wants will grow as time passes.

I feel half alive, depressed, vulnerable, frightened, emotional, disoriented and frustrated. We all have heard about the adjustments that women go through after having a baby. Whether you call it postpartum depression or baby blues; whether it lasts one day or months, it is all part of the physical and mental changes that you are going through. Some women cry for no reason, others withdraw from everything around them. There are as many different reactions as there are women. The important thing to realize is that it will probably happen to you. At this point in your life you need to feel secure, you need assurance that you are doing well. It is important that you give your body time to readjust, and that you eat right and get as much rest as possible. Another way to ease the severity of the depression is to do something for yourself. Hire a sitter. Take a bath, visit a friend, see a movie, and no matter how much you think about the baby, force yourself to stay away for at least two hours.

I'm so lonely. Often couples move right before the baby is born. There may be a good reason-more space needed or a better environment for your child. But you find yourself in a new neighborhood where you barely know anyone while you are caring for a newborn. Often, your friends and family are off pursuing careers of their own, or live far away and you must survive without the support group that women in previous generations always had. Because your husband will not be there all the time either, you must find a way to adjust to a different neighborhood, a new baby, a life without a career and your new role as a mother on your own. You may be bright and clever, but that is a lot to ask of anyone. To make matters worse, new babies sleep a great deal which makes it difficult to leave the home. If you can arrange it, hire a sitter and get out. Or invite friends who work nearby for lunch. You will find other ideas and suggestions in the chapter called "Expanding Interests".

I can't get organized. The baby is too unpredictable. Babies can't tell time. They only know to cry if they are hungry or wet or over-tired. They sleep when they feel the need, eat when they feel the need, and nothing will change that. They live on biological time. That's hard for you to get used to because you have been living by a clock for years. You went to work, left work, met appointments and attended social events according to the hands on the clock. If you fight it you'll be frustrated, panicky and bewildered. You can't win. You can struggle to make the baby obey your clock; or you can give in and live by his for awhile. Your only other alternative is to buy him a watch.

I'm so tired exhausted, fatigued and worn-down, those words and feelings are almost universal among new mothers. Why are they so tired? Lack of sleep or interrupted sleep plays a large part, and so does little contact and communication with other adults. Poor diet (eating on the run or juggling a baby with one hand and a fork with the other) can also affect your metabolism. It seems impossible to get rid of tired feelings when you have so little time and so many demands. But it can be done. Here are a few suggestions:

Sleep: Try napping when the baby does and let some of the housework go. Hire a babysitter and take a nap! If you can't do it at home without wanting to get up for the baby, go to a friend's or relative's place and rest for a while. If you have insomnia, just lay quietly with your eyes closed, that will at least bring a small amount of refreshment.

Delegate: Offer to pay a sitter a few dollars more to vacuum or dust while the baby is sleeping. Encourage your husband to help, or accept offers from friends or relatives.

Learn to relax: There are various books and articles that provide relaxation techniques. Pick up a few and try them. Even if you don't have time to read the whole book you may absorb a few helpful tips.

Find diversions: Monotony can be tiring. Force yourself to change your routine or try new things. Take a few minutes to read or think about something that stimulates your mind every day.

Exercise: You have probably heard that exercise can help you to gain energy, and it's true! It's hard to begin when there is so little spare time in the day, but force yourself to take at least ten minutes every morning. The more you manage to work it into your schedule, the more it will become a routine. It's a great way to get your adrenaline going.

Take time: That's one bit of advice that I can't stress enough. You don't think that it's possible to squeeze in any time for yourself, but it is. Other mothers have, and when they finally did, they realized how important that time really was. Your child deserves a healthy mother, and to be healthy you must have time of your own.

The Baby

Babies are moody and passionate little dictators. When they are hungry, tired or uncomfortable they want relief and they want it NOW. They have no concept of your life, the demands that you face, or the fact that you have needs and wants of your own. They only know what they want, and they call on you to provide it.

The first three to four months with a baby are similar to Army Basic Training. There are tremendous physical demands, constant orders (dictator) to follow and little time for yourself. Just as army life becomes easier after basic training, once you get through this period things will ease up. You become stronger as your body readjusts; while the baby begins to sleep through the night, follow some type of nap schedule, and reward you for your efforts with smiles of recognition that make it all worthwhile. As this phase passes, the excitement and wonder of his rapid growth will help the difficult memories of the first months to fade away. You start to have hours in the day that you can call your own. It becomes easier to get out, make plans, and become more active. A few other women share what it was like to care for a newborn:

Laura

"I seldom thought of all the physical labor involved with caring for a baby. Newborn's aren't that heavy until you have been holding your baby so long that your arm goes numb. You lift the baby up over and over again throughout the day. If you go anywhere you juggle a baby, a twenty pound diaper bag, a car seat and any other equipment you feel is necessary. You do load after load of laundry, prepare innumerable bottles and change more diapers than you'll ever care to count. I'm certainly getting one heck of a workout every day."

Gloria

"I take Susie out as often as possible. It's important for me, and I think it's good for her too. Even if she's too young to understand what she sees, she can feel different air, or the rythms of movement. She can see colors and hear sounds—there's a whole world ready to stimulate her. Some days our outings are as short as a five minute walk down the block. But it's better than nothing!"

Your Husband

He's the new father and he's going through many changes and adjustments on his own. He may feel more protective of you and the baby, and become more conscious of his own health and well-being. He might become more ambitious and responsible about his career, now that he has a child depending on him. He has also lost some of the attentions of his wife, and his home is in a constant uproar. His sleep is disturbed. He worries about the baby. He worries about you. He misses your sexual relationship. Here are three of the most common male reactions:

Eager: At some point in your pregnancy he became involved. He carefully monitored your food intake and weight, absorbed the childbirth classes and coached you through the delivery. Now that the baby is born he calls you from work several times each day to see how the baby is doing and he hurries home from work to spend time with his child. He wants to hear about every new move and development. He has plenty of his own theories about child care, which he shares often. You want him involved, but . . .

Outsider: He felt left out during the pregnancy and feels even more so now. He feels inadequate if asked to do anything for the baby, and falls apart if he's left alone to care for it. Make sure that you are not discouraging him by insisting that everything be done your own way. Let him choose his way to help or find small ways to assist you. Find ways to build his confidence. praise and encourage him as often as possible.

Rebel: For whatever reason he resents the baby, feels jealous of it, or wants to pretend like it hasn't changed anything. He believes that his meals should always be on time and that you pay the same attention to him in the evenings. Some men start drinking during this period or regress to adolescent behavior. With no attachment to the child he is experiencing all of the inconveniences without any of the benefits. Most men pass out of this phase after a few months. If the problem continues or becomes serious (excessive drinking etc.) encourage him to see a counselor. If you can, try not to let his behavior affect you too deeply. Just as some women need time to feel motherly, some men need time to feel fatherly. For many men, this doesn't come until the child is older and more responsive, more able to play.

Because the loss of your salary may have affected your budget, your husband may be working longer hours at his job, or has taken on a part-time job to help out. This leaves him fewer hours to help you or to give the baby much attention. However, it is important that he get to know his child. It will help to bond the relationship, allow him to be more tolerant of the child, and help him to appreciate what you do. He doesn't have to do a lot if time doesn't permit it. Here are a few things that dad can easily do:

- Hold, touch, smile, cuddle, or rock the baby.
- Talk, sing or read to the baby.
- Take the baby for walks in an infant carrier, stroller or backpack.

As an experienced grandfather once said, "The best thing that a father can do for his baby is to love its mother."

Your Marriage

A baby upsets everything: the relationship patterns that you are used to, your feelings about yourselves and each other, your routine, your home, and your budget. You may have already discovered that you have different ideas about child raising or child care. You must each share your time and attention with a third party. There is little time for privacy, sharing or communication. Even the best marriages feel a strain after the first child is born.

Your sexual relationship may be a point of contention at this time. Many women are not ready for sex as early as their husbands would like them to be. Even when she is physically ready she may not be mentally ready. She may be consumed with child care, tired and not yet prepared to balance the roles of wife and mother. With continued hormonal variations she may not feel sexual desire right away.

The first attempts at intercourse are sometimes painful and awkward. The wife may have trouble with lubrication, the husband with his fears of hurting her. Because you both need reassurance and security right now these problems or lack of sexual intimacy may affect your overall relationship. Your tolerance for one another thins, your frustrations grow, and you seem to be moving even further apart.

Talking about it may be difficult, but it is important that you try. Unless you are able to air your feelings and frustrations they will only compound. Get it out in the open and try to have empathy for one another's feelings. Some couples found that it helps to resume the sexual relations slowly, starting with a romantic dinner followed by a leisurely massage. Since this is seldom practical with a new baby around, hire a babysitter and go out for the evening. A motel room may provide a better, more neutral (no baby things) environment as you rediscover this intimate part of your relationship.

Your Mother

After you have your first baby you may find that your relationship with your mother will change. Perhaps you feel that you now understand her better, or that you understand her less than before. Usually, whatever your general relationship is with your mom, it will intensify after you become a parent yourself. A few women share some of their feelings:

Fran

"I was so afraid that I would be like my mother. She was extremely over-protective, almost smothering. Even now I find myself backing away when she gets too close. That was one of the reasons I was so afraid to give up my job. I didn't want to stay home and make my baby my whole life. The surprise is that she has changed. She is so relaxed and laid back around Charlie that it amazes me. It helped me to realize that I won't necessarily be the same way that she was, and I can relax and be myself. Most importantly, I have finally begun to understand her better now that I feel so protective of my own child."

Lois
"My mother had plenty of advice. She considered herself an authority on children. She had suggestions about everything from how to wash the baby's sheets to how often I should rock him. I tried to integrate my own ideas with hers—after all she had raised five children. But just once I wish she would have saidYou are doing a good job."

You carry certain attitudes about your childhood, as well as your new ideas for child raising. There's a good chance that some of these will conflict with the way that your mother raised you. Some mothers are hurt by this and see it as a rejection of their mothering. "You turned out okay" she might tell you. What can you do to resolve the situation? Unless it gets out of hand (then talk about it) you probably won't have to do anything. You see, your mom is going through her own period of adjustment, especially if this is her first grandchild. A new baby reminds her of her own days as a new mother. It's an experience that she now wants to share because you are better able to empathize. If she sees you doing something differently than she did, she wants you to know "this other way worked for me". There are times when she may be right, and times when you know better. There are periods when you find her advice helpful and reassuring, and others where it is extremely frustrating. Try not to get defensive, a suggestion is not necessarily criticism. You needn't reject it out of hand or accept it as absolute truth. Weigh it with the rest of the knowledge you've acquired, check it against your own instincts, then do what you think is right.

Deep down, your mother understands that you won't accept everything that she says. She knows that this is your child and that you will make mistakes, just as she did. She'll say what she believes, and you'll say what you believe, but the ultimate decisions are yours to make. If she goes to far, let her know. Once the boundaries are set you should fall into a comfortable balance. Unless you have totally rejected your upbringing, you will probably follow the same basic style of parenting that your mother did. Just as you incorporated some of her best recipes into your meals, you will take what is best from her mothering and add a little of your own.

Another woman shares some of the problems she faced as a new mother:

Teresa

"It was so hard. I was scared and anxious about doing things the right way. I didn't have any confidence in myself and I was overwhelmed by the fact that this baby's life depended on me. My mother never said much of anything. If I would ask for her opinion she would say 'well it depends on the baby'. She was no help at all. I had never spent much time around children and I felt so helpless. I know that millions of other women had managed to raise children, but for some reason it was hard for me to cope. Finally, I asked my mother-in-law for help. She stepped right in and started visiting me every day. She advised me on how to dress, bathe, feed, diaper and hold the baby. She had very strong ideas on how long he should cry, what laundry detergent I should use and everything else you could think of. At first I meekly accepted her views, she certainly had more experience than I did. But as time passed I began to develop my own ideas, which sometimes clashed with hers. I had begun to get a feel for Tina's personality and there were times that I knew I was right. Finally one day, I said 'I appreciate your help, but this is my baby and I have learned enough to care for her now.' She wasn't very happy, but at least I had snapped out of my insecurity and lethargy."

In Summary

A child is a tremendous responsibility. It requires love, attention, and the surrender of some of your freedom and independence. You may decide to put aside a career that brought you satisfaction in order to give more of yourself to your child. You allow a new life to take time and attention from your marriage. You make an enormous lifetime commitment to care for another human being.

A child can bring a feeling of teamwork to your marriage that can help to deepen and intensify your relationship. You share struggles and pleasures and a wonderful feeling of accomplishment.

A child can help you to grow and to find qualities of character in yourself that you never knew you had. It stretches your capacity for giving and teaches you kindness and patience. You become less self-absorbed and develop greater maturity that can solidify your purpose and direction in life.

Homemaker

I never wanted to be a housewife. They were people who went to the supermarket with curlers in their hair and always did the laundry on Tuesday. They changed from their bathrobe to flowered dresses around noon—just in time to watch the daily soap operas. At parties, they talked about things like their children's bowel movements. They went on game shows and screeched when they won refrigerators, and were obsessed with clean toilets and ring-around-the-collar.

Today, I am one of those women who stay at home. Not only is the aforementioned image totally inapplicable to my lifestyle, the truth is that the stereotypical housewife is extinct. The new breed of homemaker is a diverse group, with a large number of them being former career women themselves. One may be a 38 year old former executive who has just had her first child, another might be a 26 year old former teacher with a busy toddler. With such a variety of ages and backgrounds they often share only one common trait—they have decided to stay at home to raise their own children and strengthen the family bond.

These women are well aware of the poor image they receive from the rest of society. Many even shared such attitudes themselves when they worked. In spite of this, most are enthusiastic about their decision. They believe that in some ways their lives are privileged because they have an opportunity to enjoy their family, their home environment, and themselves on a full-time basis. They are aware that homemaking, like all other life choices, can have its drawbacks. Yet, they have found a way to overcome their problems and create their own happiness while receiving little esteem from the outside world. There are times, however, when they continue to be frustrated by the attitudes that some people express toward their occupation. A few shared their sentiments:

Audrey

"A few months ago I had to pick up a business associate of my husband's from the airport. We made small talk on the way back, and eventually he asked me what I did. I had been waiting for that question, because I had finally designed a great answer to it! I told him 'My job is an exciting challenge every day—I work with children.' That made him chuckle. 'What I try to do' I continued, 'is create a stimulating environment using music, literature, art and physical activities to encourage their individual growth, exploration and talents.' He was obviously interested. 'Are you a teacher?' he asked. I shook my head. 'Guess again' I said. 'I've got it, you run a daycare center!' he exclaimed. 'Almost' I answered with a smile. 'I'm a full-time mother.' You could see the light go out. 'Is that all you do?' he said."

Tricia

"Most writers become frustrated by the attitudes of would-be authors. They are people who seem to think that if they only had the time, they could easily write books, stories, or magazine articles as well as anyone. Because they have never tried to write, they have no appreciation for the discipline that it requires. They cannot comprehend what grueling work writing and rewriting can be. Homemakers have the same problem. To someone on the outside looking in, it seems that we just sit around all day, occasionally straightening up the house or telling the kids to change the channel on the television. It looks so simple and easy that they assume that anyone who does it full-time must be lazy, and not require much mental stimulation. They have no idea of how much creativity it takes to run a home, bring up children, and still find time for your own interests."

Kate

"Why should other people's opinions even matter to us? We live in a society where people see nothing wrong with paying the movie stars and athletes who entertain us millions of dollars each year. But when the teachers who help to educate the next generation, or policemen who protect our lives and property ask for a small pay raise—the newspapers and town halls are filled with complainers. They are only angry because those salaries come out of their budget in a more recognizable way. We seem to place so little value on the things that should be most important. It shouldn't surprise any of us that although we do the most to maintain a healthy family life, we receive such little esteem."

Sally

"I wish the media and all of the other groups who do so much to influence people's attitudes would devote more attention to homemaking as a valid option for women. It seems like all of the entertainment programs that feature families have both parents pursuing careers—and some type of loveable mother substitute for the children. Not only is this portrayal unrealistic, it is disappointing that they would rather show substitute mothers than the real thing. In talk shows and magazines the problems and needs of working mothers are always stressed. What about us? No one seems to want to acknowledge our existence any more. I know that women who choose homemaking are a minority, but there are still millions of us out here! And just as I want my daughters to know that it is acceptable to strive to be a doctor or an investment banker, it would be nice if they could also consider homemaking as a valid career choice.''

Carolyn

''My former college roommate is a lawyer. She is divorced, has two daughters and a live-in housekeeper/ nanny. Although we had sporadically kept in touch, I hadn't seen her in years. Recently, I paid a visit and I was stunned by her family life. The children weren't at breakfast 'so that I can prepare for the day in peace' she explained. Before she left for work she spent exactly ten minutes with them. Twelve hours later she was home. Her daughters had already eaten, and while we were sitting in the living room the nanny brought them in. The whole scene was so stiff it reminded me of something in a nineteenth century Victorian novel. After exactly twenty minutes of attention, the children were led away. I looked at her. 'Is that all the time that you spend with them every day?' I asked. 'Oh no' she said. 'After dinner I'll go up and read them a story for twenty minutes, then tuck them in.' 'I guess you make up for it on weekends' I ventured. 'Of course!' she replied. 'Their father has them on Saturdays, and I always spend six hours with them on Sunday—that's our quality day' she said proudly. Then she caught my incredulous look. 'Hey, I work a twelve hour day!' she said. 'Then I usually have two or three hours of work to do in the evening. I'm doing the best that I can, and the children have nanny to keep them occupied.'

'But you're their mother!' I said. 'They grow up so quickly, how can you schedule them in and out of your life like a dental appointment?' 'Don't lay that guilt stuff on me' she answered. 'I give them my undivided

attention in those periods. They know how to reach me
if I am really needed.' 'Couldn't you work fewer
hours?' I asked. 'Why should I?' she responded. 'My
job is important to me, what I do helps other people. In
any case, I've worked hard to get to this point, I'm not
going to let anyone hurt it now. Let's face it. In another
ten to fifteen years the girls will be gone, and I'll be on
my own. I would like to be a full partner by then. I'll
have my own life, and plenty to fill my time.'

It was all so incredibly sad to me. I ended up cutting
my visit short because I couldn't help but think that if
I wasn't there she might spend a few minutes more
with them. I couldn't imagine growing up in that kind
of atmosphere, and I often think of those little girls.''

Homemakers today firmly believe that their lifestyle is
important, and they are willing to make sacrifices in order to
stay home with their families. In a *Parent's* magazine survey
(7/83), in which women were asked how they would
respond to increased financial pressure, ''79% said they
would economize on the household budget, 78% would cut
back on personal expenses, (and) 70% would save on their
social life and vacations''. These women clearly value what
they are doing. In fact a Better Homes & Gardens survey of
''How work is affecting American families'' (2/82), shows
that a higher percentage of homemakers are happier with
their jobs than women who are employed outside the home.
A few other women share their beliefs:

Rachel
''A family needs a base or a core to start from, and
I don't care how many surveys or studies contradict me
about this. If there is no one to hold it all together and
co-ordinate the home and family, everyone in the home
will begin to lead separate lives. That takes away from
the strong bond that families should have. My children
may not appreciate the fact that I am always here for

them now, but they will later. I know how secure I felt knowing that my mom was always ready to hear my latest triumph or tragedy, and I want my children to grow up with the same feeling, I'm shaping an atmosphere of calm and stability for us all—and what could be more important or challenging than that?''

Melanie

''I was talking with a former co-worker one day. She told me that she would never understand why I gave up my career to stay at home. 'It's simple' I told her, 'I wanted to stop spreading myself so thin, and enjoy my family and my own life.' 'But you didn't have to give up your career to do that' she answered. 'I'm doing it all now, and I know it isn't easy, but I have managed to balance everything fairly well.'

The company we worked for had an annual performance evaluation in which we were required to examine our own performance and goals. A part of that evaluation was establishing the percentage of the time and effort that you devoted to the different parts of your job. I was curious to see how she managed this balancing act, so I challenged her to give me the percentages of her time that she devoted to the different aspects of her life. She asked me to do the same. We created five categories, with a final catch-all group that we referred to as 'Other'. That covered housework, entertainment, shopping, time with family and friends, etc. This is what we came up with:

	Dana	Mel
Career	45%	1%
Marriage	5%	17%
Children	35%	52%
Self	3%	14%
Other	12%	16%

We were both a little surprised by our figures. 'My life isn't perfect' I told her. 'But as you can see, I can devote more time to myself and my family than you can. In your life, no one is getting a fair share, in fact your career receives more attention than your children, marriage, and yourself combined. Is your job that important to you?'

'Not really' she answered. 'But you know how hard we have to work to keep up, much less to get ahead.' I do what I can, when I can, to keep everybody happy.'

'But that's my point' I told her. 'If you strip away all of the justifications and excuses it boils down to this. You can do enough just to *get by* in everything, or you can concentrate your efforts on what is most important to you, and do it right. The difference is the same as the distinction between the family eating frozen dinners from the microwave or a home-cooked meal from scratch. They both serve the same purpose—filling everyone's stomachs. But one is obviously more desirable, and more beneficial for the family itself.'

'I see what you are saying' she said. 'Yet, I can't agree. Why should I be the one to provide everyone else's needs? My needs are important too.' 'You're right' I said. 'Lets compare our percentages. Which one of us is spending more time on ourself?' She didn't say anything, so I went on. 'If you add the 45% from your career to your *Self* category that would give you 48% for yourself and 40% for your husband and children. Does that describe things more accurately?' 'No, but let's drop it' she said. 'I have to do some thinking.'

A few months later she called to let me know that she had resigned. 'I decided to take some time to re-evaluate my priorities and my future' she said. I'm glad that she is giving herself the time. Don't think that I was on a campaign to drive women from the work force. I just wish every woman would take a hard look at their priorities, and then give those things the time that they deserve.''

Ellen

''I'm a gambler. I have risked my personal resources, my time, talent, and energy on a small group of people. Why? Because I believe in the importance of home and family, and that children should be raised by their own mothers. Just as with any career, this role requires certain important qualifications. You need courage and spirit to overlook other people's attitudes and create a whole new lifestyle on your own. You must have stamina and tenacity to continue doing your job, despite the boredom and repetition of it. You must be innovative—find ways to help yourself and each family member grow individually and contribute to the family as a whole. You must be calm and not easily perturbed—even when four eight-year-olds have put the dog on the roof. Most of all, you must have confidence in the importance of your role. Home-making is not an easy job, and it's a risk that many women are afraid to take. The truth is, only the best and the brightest need apply.''

Sarah

''I see myself as an artist. I produce a warm and loving environment for my family, and I create a suitable background for each individual's needs. I induce the excitement of special occasions with food, decoration and traditions. I provide harmony and balance for the misfortunes and delights that pass through our home every day. My attitude and outlook sets the tone for our surroundings in the same way that a painting can tie together all of the elements in a room. It's not always easy to maintain unity and accord, but that is all part of the challenge.''

Joyce

"Making a home for your family isn't just a matter of paying for it, decorating it, and cleaning it. It is providing the warmth, love, and security that every person needs to have in their life. It's impossible to have these qualities regularly available if both parents work full-time outside of the home. Instead the family has a glimpse of this warmth and closeness for a few moments each day, or a hint of what their lives *could* be like during occasional weekends and vacations. But there is little time for them to savor these qualities because there is always a mountain of work in the background awaiting completion. It almost seems cruel to have a taste of something that you crave, then have it snatched away again."

Elizabeth

"Think about the monks in the Dark Ages. At first glance their role seemed superficial. What value could there be for an intelligent person to enter a monastery and to opt for a lifestyle so different from that of the rest of the world? Yet, some of those men were writers whose thinking has influenced generations. Many of them spent their days copying books. They passed on knowledge in a time when there was little reverence for scholarship. Some historians believe that their actions may have saved Western civilization.

Our lifestyle may seem just as hollow and incomprehensible to many people today. Yet we homemakers are diligently focusing on the importance of humans over things in a materialistic society. We are preserving a concept of home and family that future generations may thank us for."

Renee

"I have a sister who is much older than I am. She continued working after her children were born because she wanted them to be assured of all of the good things in life—a nice home, summer camp, and college educations. Because both she and her husband had to travel a great deal in their work, the children spent much of their time with an amalgamation of daycare centers, neighbors, and relatives.

They had good intentions. They talked incessantly of the family vacations they would take, but the years flew by and there was never a right time for them both to get away. Both she and her husband have achieved their career goals after all of those years of hard work. Their children are grown and out of college. They have all gone their separate ways. My sister often complains bitterly that they seldom call or visit. To me, it's apparant that there are few bonds among them, and no feeling of roots.

I realize that not all families with working mothers end up that way. But seeing this one so close to home convinced me that what you get out of your family life is exactly what you put into it."

Marie

"The children scramble for their lunch boxes and books and hurry out the door to the waiting bus. Up and down the block I see crisply dressed men and women marching to their cars to flee our tree-lined streets for the exacting world of work. Soon the sounds of car engines and children's shouts have all died away. Everything is still, tranquil and silent. I am alone on the block.

My time is my own. I can watch the clock if I wish to, perhaps I'll hurry from one task to another so that I will have time to drive to the next town and meet my sister for lunch. Or I might curl up with a good book and remain oblivious to the hours as they tick away. Of course there are days when the demands of others will dictate my schedule. I have to wait for the dishwasher repairman when I would rather complete my grocery shopping, or drive the children to their various activities when I would prefer to work on my needlepoint. Yet, there is seldom a day when I cannot liberate an hour or two, just for me.

My life is free. Not necessarily the freedom *from* harrying demands and exacting schedules; but the freedom *to* pursue my own pleasures, and spend most of my hours in the way that I prefer. I can begin each day in surroundings that I choose. If it's dark, dreary, gloomy and rainy I can pull the drapes, turn on the light and snugly stay indoors. If there is bright sunshine, blue sky and a fresh, gentle breeze I can throw open the windows and let the exhilarating air fill my home.

My lifestyle is shared with millions of women from previous generations. The things that they thought were important—enjoyable surroundings, home-cooked meals, family togetherness, children, laughter, books, solitude and a happy marriage are equally essential to me. In fact, they are so important that I want to spend my days ensuring that they are present in our home on a regular basis.

Today was a beautiful sunny day. I pulled the lawn chair closer to my flower garden and had lunch while I enjoyed the many colors glimmering in the bright light. I let the peace soothe me, a touch of their fragrance refresh me. I felt in touch with the rythms of life. By having calm days like this I can maintain an inner serenity that helps me to soothe the ruffled feelings of a child not invited to a party, or the tired frustration of a husband battling fierce competition at his office. They know that they can find a haven for their troubles in the familiar and loving environment that we call home.

If I were to leave every morning and join my army of neighbors in their quest for money and status, there would be no one left. No one to run to school with

forgotten books, or to take in a neighbor's child who can't find his key. No one to enjoy the flowers, the sunshine, the hum of each day that would continue without an audience. Once, I was a part of the working world. I would rush home tired of the daily grind, hectically
preparing dinner and listening to the children. Trying to catch snatches of pleasure in between moments of sheer fatigue. It has taught me to appreciate my present life even more. If I had the money, I would pay to be a homemaker!''

Confucius said that ''The strength of a nation is derived from the integrity of its homes.'' How do these words affect us today? In the same period where less importance was placed on family life, and more emphasis was given to self-fulfillment, when a large percentage of our families were split apart by divorce—we saw our national fiber begin to weaken—morally, ethically, and financially.

Each family is the bedrock for our civilization, a reflection of society as a whole. As those individuals in each family leave the home and take their places in our schools, corporations, factories, and government, they will transform those institutions with the attitudes, values, and deficiencies they have acquired. If a family does not provide a stable base for our principles, where will the members receive them? Television? Schools? The neighbors? A concerted effort must be made in one place—the home—to preserve the ideals that our country was founded upon.

In our complex society, our homes are the last place where privacy and simplicity reign. Where we can step back from the clamor and demands of numerous obligations and put them into perspective. It is our hedge against the powerlessness that we often feel as we are overwhelmed by those other claims. If a home becomes nothing more than a hotel, where family members meet in passing, then the people in it will begin to search elsewhere for their basic needs of warmth,

understanding, comfort, support and security. With someone there to shape the environment, the home becomes a
place to return to, to relax in; a haven from the other pressures in life. Such an atmosphere can only be woven with
love and stability. Like all relationships, the family must be
nourished through communication, activity and traditions
shared on a regular basis.

Your Marriage

Until now your relationship was based on easily measurable contributions. You both left your home every day and went to jobs where you faced similar problems and received comparable rewards. Once you become a home-maker, all of this changes. The functions that you perform will no longer be parallel, and your rewards will be set by the value that you each place on your contribution. In a way, you will be refashioning your lives together. Here are some of the problems that you may have to deal with:

You no longer share the housework. When you both worked your husband probably pitched in to some degree and helped with the household chores. Now, they are your responsibility. On the one hand, since you are at home full-time it seems fair to expect you to handle the cleaning and upkeep. On the other hand, few people enjoy the boredom and repetition of housework. In addition, you may find that your husband's standards and attitudes toward house-keeping have changed. One woman explains:

"When I worked, my husband did the laundry. Occasionaly we had a load where the colors ran together, or a favorite outfit of mine had been shrunk. But I said very little because I appreciated his contribution. Now, he's become a perfectionist. If a shirt he wants to wear isn't cleaned, or if I hang one up

the wrong way and it gets wrinkled, he has a fit. If I
point out his past errors, his only response is 'that
wasn't my job'. It's extraordinarily frustrating, but I
guess it comes with the territory.''

Subtle shifts in power. You no longer have the economic
clout that your income gave you. Suddenly you must rely on
someone else for your support, and that isn't easy to deal
with when you are used to being independent. You've lost
the financial freedom that would allow you to walk away if
you wanted to, and it's frightening to become more reliant
on the success of your marriage for your future stability.
These attitudes, and similar ones that your husband now
feels, can affect the way that you relate to one another. He
has the paycheck, you have the home environment you both
desire, and you must find new common ground to recreate
the balance between you. The key to it all is the value that
you each place on your function as a homemaker. If you both
hold the role that you play in high esteem it will naturally be
easier to maintain equality in your relationship.

The need for control. We all require areas that we can
regulate and govern with absolute authority in our lives. You
may have been able to use your job as an outlet for your need
for authority, and that can be especially hazardous now. You
may be competing with your husband in areas that you
previously left alone. In addition, there is a tendency for
homemakers to consider the home as 'their turf', and you
may find that this attitude can cause conflict in your
marriage. In most marriages, the following areas can be
battlegrounds for power and control:

- Handling the finances.
- Raising the children.
- Taking on new responsibilities.
- Planning for the future.
- Making major purchases.
- Spending most of the money.

- Caring for the home.
- Planning social activities.

Are you uncertain as to where your strongest need for control is? Then ask yourself "What would make me feel the most threatened?" "When is it crucial that I have the final say?"

As you realign your roles you can find ways to mediate these struggles. For example: If you both feel the need to be in charge of the family's financial affairs you may be able to compromise. One solution would be to divide that function. Perhaps one of you could take charge of the day-to-day expenses while the other would handle your savings and investments. It will take time and effort from both of you, but unless you resolve these conflicts they will serve as a hidden base for other disagreements.

More time together. "Wait a minute!" you're thinking. "That's one of the reasons I'm staying home!" You are right. With more time to devote to your marriage, your relationship will certainly improve. Yet, you will have to deal with each other's initial expectations and the patterns you have formed until now. Two other women explain:

Marilyn
"I think we both assumed that once I stayed home our evenings together would be idyllic. I would have all day to take care of the house and the twins. Then in the evening we would sip champagne and chat by the fire. It isn't that easy. Since they are still babies, they don't always fall asleep when the clock chimes seven, nor do they sleep the whole night through! But maybe when they're older . . . "

Angela
"When I was working we tried to make every minute that we had together count. Once I was home and we had the extra time to talk, or just sit in the same room

and read or watch television, it seemed wrong or
awkward to separate. If I really wanted to go and
telephone a friend, or he preferred to tinker in his
workshop, we kept quiet because we didn't want the
other one to think that we were abandoning them. We
are slowly getting used to the idea that undivided
attention isn't always required."

A Better Marriage

A survey of 41,000 readers of Parents (7/83) indicated that
"more than half of full-time homemakers believe that their
marriages are better because they are at home full-time".
Once most women adjust to the new lifestyle of homemaking, both they and their husbands are pleasantly
surprised at how much the change has helped to improve
their relationship. Most men when interviewed freely admit
that they are happiest when their wives are satisfied and at
peace with themselves. They enjoy an orderly home, and do
not like the idea of taking any large responsibility for its
upkeep. They like to feel that their children are well cared
for, and prefer that their wife provide them with attention
and nurturing. Because a homemaker has more time to
devote to them, she is more likely to meet this male ideal. I
am not for one moment advocating that women return to
revolving their lives around their husbands. But as we all
know, when they are happy, it makes our lives easier. A few
other women explain the difference staying home has made
to their marriage:

Lorraine

"When I was working, a typical day began with a
scramble for the shower and an argument over who
should have started the coffee. We gulped our breakfast
while we traded schedules and tasks to be done, and
struggled to get ourselves and the children dressed.
Then a quick kiss and we were out the door, dashing

in different directions. In the evening we would snap at each other as we rushed to make dinner, straighten up the house, and try and spend time with the children. We would have a short period to bring each other up on the latest news, then we'd collapse into bed. Sometimes we even had enough energy for sex. Occasionally we would arrange a private weekend away from home. However, there was always an unspoken agreement to keep them enjoyable and avoid conflict as much as possible. There was seldom the time to nourish our relationship, or simply relax without a clock ticking in the back of our minds.

Now we can appreciate our time together, and still feel comfortable pursuing our own individual interests. Breakfast will never be calm with three children, but the atmosphere is more relaxed and less hurried. Although we still discuss tasks that must be completed, he can also take a few moments and mention what he's looking forward to or worried about on his job that day. I listen to him and the children, and because I know that I'll have time to myself shortly, I can give them my full attention. In the evening, dinner is ready when he comes home, and there is no the rush to get things done. He can spend time alone with the children while I straighten up, or we can do family things together without worrying about chores. We are both less tired in the evening—he doesn't help around the house during the week so it has taken some of the pressure off of him. I have created my own schedule, and can pretty well keep to it and have plenty of free time. So we have more time to talk, be romantic, or just enjoy quiet companionship once the children are in bed.

Staying at home has also given me more of an opportunity to think about our relationship, and I share my new insights with him when I have a chance. Our marriage is now the best it has ever been, and it's getting better all the time.''

How Men See It

Men have had plenty of adjustments to make in the last thirty years. In the previous generation a man was made to feel that he was a failure if his wife worked. He was seen as someone who was unable to support and care for his family on his own. Today, men like, and even expect the extra income that their wife can provide, and enjoy the way that a second income eases the pressures and responsibilities he feels towards the family. Yet, they still feel the pull of their own childhood, and would like their wives to give the children and themselves the attention a full-time homemaker can provide.

How do men feel when their wives become homemakers? Most have mixed emotions, and their answers depend on how much they had counted on their wife's income, and how long it has been since the change took place. Here, a few share their views:

Bob

"My wife has become more independent since she left work and had our son. She used to be too tired or busy to talk out many decisions with me, and often left the resolution of problems up to me. Now she has developed strong ideas about our future, and is more interested in how we plan our lives. I'm glad. I didn't like going it alone. That left me solely responsible for any mistakes, and I had always wanted our marriage to be a partnership. Because she has more time now, she can think about my ideas, and sometimes come up with better solutions. I'm proud of her, she's a good mother, a wonderful wife, and it means a lot to me that she has put aside her career for our child."

Tom

"There are times when I am jealous. It would be nice to not have to go to work every day. You don't have to dress up. You can sleep in if there's a blizzard. You can stay outdoors when the weather is nice. You can control your own time, and you only have to answer to yourself. At other times I feel guilty. I know it isn't easy being tied to the house caring for children. It must be hard spending your days doing housework that gets undone as soon as you complete it. My wife is a vibrant, intelligent woman and it can't be easy for her to adapt those qualities to this new lifestyle. There is little I can do about it, except to try and be supportive. I know that I am not always as understanding and helpful as she would like me to be, but I try. I remind her as often as possible that when the children are a little older, she will have more freedom to pursue other activities."

Daniel

"At first I resented my wife's decision to stay at home. It seemed unfair that she could choose, but I couldn't. Women really have the best of both worlds. They can go out and be dynamos in the workforce, yet when they get tired of it they can quit. In addition, where I work it's almost a status symbol to have a wife in a high-powered job bringing in a hefty income. Now that she is staying at home I have the feeling that some of my co-workers see her as a little less important, less intelligent than their own wives. That bothered me for awhile, but I decided that there may be some jealousy hidden behind their disdain. As time passed, I also changed my attitude about my wife staying at home. Now that we've come out of the initial period of adjustment I can look around and see the benefits. Our son is very happy and well-adjusted, it's obvious that he is thriving in her care. I enjoy coming home to a clean house and dinner on the table. Now we feel like a real family, I hadn't realized how much I missed that feeling when I was growing up. Today I see my co-workers and their wives in a different light. They are all so busy chasing the status quo, they don't have time to realize what they are missing."

Rick

"My wife wants it all. She can stay home and be a housewife, but demands that she maintain her independence and be treated equally. If you ask me, the relationship is very unequal. I'm supposed to happily support everyone, and never complain about how the money is spent. She wants me to feel guilty when she's unfulfilled, and boost her spirits when she is depressed. Yet, when I voice my opinion, or ask for attention in return—I'm being the selfish one!"

Improving Your Marriage

Your marriage is a lifetime commitment, and it deserves your time and attention. Just as you were willing to make sacrifices and compromises for your career, you must be equally willing to grant your relationship the same amount of effort. One woman compares the principles of marriage and career:

"Your life together can run as smoothly as any successful corporation, or fall into as much trouble as a failing one, depending on how you go about it. Every relationship requires the following traits: good interpersonal communications, participative management, flexibility, loyalty, long range planning, and a commitment to completing objectives. Just as you ensured that you portrayed these values in the work force, you should make the effort to apply them to your marriage to make it a success."

Here are some other concepts that are important in a happy marriage:

Confidence in the ultimate success of the relationship. It provides a feeling that helps you to ride out the bad times and wait for the good.

Commitment to the permanence of the relationship. You will not give up without a fight.

Compromise, which is the ability to accept some elements that you dislike for the value of others that you enjoy.

Trust in your spouse's commitment to the relationship, and in your belief that you can be open and vulnerable without rejection.

Mutual dependence because you are each a source in fulfilling the other's needs.

Companionship in knowing that you like each other, and You enjoy spending time together.

Shared values since your outlooks, morals, and goals are generally compatible.

Traditions which are the time you spend together in laughter, anger, joy, and tears that help to cement your bond.

The basis for all good relationships is communication. Married couples are often distracted by so many other concerns that they fail to take the time to communicate their deepest thoughts, feelings and needs to one another. The basics of good communication are sometimes forgotten, it might help to reconsider them here:

- Set aside a time that will have a minimal amount of interruptions.
- Talk about your feelings, frustrations, anxieties, hopes, dreams, ideas and needs.
- Try to avoid talking about trivial topics.
- Listen to what your partner says, give him your undivided attention. Insist that he do the same for you.
- Before you respond make sure you clearly understand what your spouse is saying. When you are not sure, ask.
- Don't make accusations or put one another on the

defensive. Say what you think, and believe it and leave it at that.
- *Ask for a response*
  What do you think about this?
  How does this make you feel?
  What do you think we should do?
- At times when you feel distant or angry with one another, write out your feelings. Don't be afraid to express negative ones, or try to edit yourself. Then express your understanding, your love and forgiveness. Share it with your spouse.
- When things are icy between you, pick one of the sentences below and complete it with a compliment. It's hard to be angry with someone who is being so nice.
  One of the things I enjoy about you is . . .
  I admire you because . . .
  I appreciate it when . . .
  One thing I love about our relationship is . . .
  One thing I love about you is . . .

Keeping Your Love Alive

Even if we are communicating well, we all have times when our marriage could use some romance and excitement. Here are some ideas to consider:

- Thank your spouse for something he or she has done, today or in the past. This gives you both a warm feeling, and helps to renew the relationship.
- Make a date, a rendezvous with each other. promise not to talk about anything humdrum, just each other, as you did when you were dating.
- Take time each year, to make a 'state of the union' message on your marriage relationship. Discuss where you have failed, how you have improved, and what steps you can take to do better next year.
- Go out of your way to express affection; show it with

kisses, hugs, and compliments.
- Take time to commemorate the past you share. Talk about moments that made your relationship special—when did you know that 'this was the person you wanted to marry?' What special dates did you have? Uproarious moments? Take out photo albums and relive experiences with each other.
- Make anniversaries and birthdays special celebrations. Give personal, special gifts. Create new traditions and celebrations to share.
- Visit places you would like to live, and talk about your dreams.
- Discover new places, such as new neighborhoods, restaurants or parks—together.
- Be sentimental. Pick your spouse up at work, as if it were a date.
- Recall a favorite date and 'return to the scene'.
- Talk about the romantic things you would like your spouse to do. What was your most romantic moment? (If you cannot think of one, what is your fantasy of one?)

Here are some ideas for your sexual relationship:

- Change locations.
- Play out fantasies.
- Bathe/shower together.
- Make love when the mood strikes.
- Reverse roles.
- Be playful.
- Break your routine.
- Take time to think of yourself as a sexual partner.
- Create surprises.
- Make your bedroom sexy, with soft lights, music, etc. Ban sex for a while and just cuddle.
- Take a mini vacation.
- Give up something else that you spend time on (such

as watching television) and use that time for sex.

• Create excitement by telling your spouse ahead of time what will happen later.

Look over these lists and select five things that you would like to do. Feel free to add your own ideas. Then ask your spouse to do the same. After you have compared lists, you can take turns doing them.

What Is Marriage?

It is knowing that your happiness isn't guaranteed, but tryir ; for it anyway. It is trusting your spouse and your love enough to ride out the rocky and difficult times. It is learning to understand and accept your partner's outlook, even when you don't agree with it. It is having the freedom to open up and share your love, your thoughts and feelings without fear of being hurt. it is a sense of belonging, companionship, and security. It is laughter and tears, inside jokes and playfulness, and the joy of loving and being loved.

There are times in every marriage when it seems easier, even more attractive to give up and walk away. The real difference between a good and a bad marriage is that in the good ones—no one walks. If you make your spouse and your marriage number one in your life; if you make an effort to give as well as to receive; and if you allow your relationship to continually grow along with yourselves, you can have a successful marriage.

Living With Less Money

You wouldn't have left your job if you weren't sure that you would find a way to manage without your salary. You may have spent hours with your calculator creating a precise budget; or just have a rough plan to cut back a little bit in each spending area. Whatever the case, you are going to discover that the transition will be more difficult than you expected it to be. You can count on using a great deal of patience, flexibility, and inventiveness while you adapt to these new financial circumstances. As you may have anticipated, your expenses in some areas will decrease. Here are a few that you can count on:

Food: Lunches, fast foods, frozen dinners and restaurant meals can all be cut out or cut back.

Clothing: Of course you will still buy clothes, but homemakers don't need $200 dresses on their jobs.

Transportation: No more travel back and forth to work.

Child care: You will still want to hire a babysitter occasionally, but it is no longer necessary to pay for everyday care.

Home upkeep: If you have been paying someone else to care for your home there is a good chance that you will drop that service now.

Minor repairs: You or your husband will have the time to

145

	complete them instead of hiring someone else.
Taxes:	You may have more spendable income if the loss of your salary will also lower your tax bracket.

The effect that the loss of your paycheck has on your standard of living depends a great deal upon how much of your income was needed to meet the major bills, such as the mortgage payment or rent. In addition, your expectations for your new lifestyle can make your adjustment easier or more difficult. If you continue to try to maintain the spending habits that you had with two incomes, you are obviously going to run into trouble somewhere along the line.

A few other women talk about the frustrations that they faced:

Vanessa

"Although I knew that we would have to cut back when I stopped working, the impact of what that meant didn't hit me at first. I was used to buying what I pleased when I went shopping. If I saw something that I liked, I bought it. If I went to the grocery store, I just pulled whatever I wanted off the shelves. Suddenly, I was living on a tight budget. I had to make a list before I went to the store, estimating what each item would cost. If my list was longer than my budget, I would have to juggle things around—or do without until the next week. It made me so nervous! I would walk through the store with my stomach in knots and my palms sweaty, wielding my calculator and list. I was terrified of the embarassment that not having enough money at the checkout might bring. As time passed, I became better at balancing my money with what I needed to buy. But living on a budget can still be frustrating and upsetting. We are certainly more fortunate than many people, but this has given me a tiny glimpse of what real poverty must feel like. I am more grateful that we are able to buy what we need, and try to keep that perspective when I get exasperated. If I could do it again, I think I would have taken it more slowly and started this budget before I stopped working. It would have helped to ease the transition, and to make me more confident about what I am doing now.''

Kay

"When we were tired of the snow and cold, we could throw our clothes in a bag and go to the Caribbean. Even if we didn't go, we knew that we could if we wanted to. After completing a job successfully, I could reward myself with a shopping spree. If we thought our marriage could use a change, we could splurge on a night on the town, or a weekend getaway. We never worried about money—we had what we needed, when we needed it.

What a change! At first, it was very painful to realize that the money was no longer there. We felt locked into a lifestyle without luxurious extras. But with more time on my hands, I was able to find creative substitutes. One day in mid-winter I surprised my husband with an indoor picnic. We laid out blankets, brought out the sunlamp, put on our bathing suits and used our imagination. For special effects I played a record that had ocean sounds that I had found at the library. It was a lot of fun, and after awhile you could almost smell the water!

Sometimes I treat myself to a shopping trip when I really need a lift, or when I've been working extra hard. I can't spend the way that I used to, but since I love to read and listen to music, I'll spend a great deal of time selecting the right book or tape for my current mood. I find I'm more careful about what I buy, and that I value it more. When our relationship could use a lift, we'll go out to simpler places—maybe a drive to the lake and a stop at a local pub for a few drinks, or just window shopping as we stroll around town. We actually talk more on these excursions, and it's similar to how we spent our time when we were dating in college. We are 'less secure monetarily, but more secure in our relationship than ever before.

If I would have heard someone say these things while I was working I would have thought—'how that poor woman is deluding herself!', but I don't think that I am. You can truly find pleasure in small things if you open yourself to them, and now you have the time to elicit more enjoyment from all things.''

There are many ways to save money, and when you were working you may not have had time to think about or implement many of them. Here are a few ideas to consider:

- If you haven't stopped working yet, it's a good idea to begin living without your income as soon as possible. It may not be realistic to do this completely because you probably use more money right now, but slowly cut back as much as possible. Try to curb your spending habits and avoid impulsive purchases.
- Each time you bring out your wallet or credit card, think. Ask yourself, ''Do I really need this, or am I just spending money because it's in my purse?'' Many of us spend more money in our last few months of working thinking that if we don't buy it now, we probably never will. While that could be true, you may discover that had you put the money aside, you would have been able to buy something of greater importance to you at a time when you really needed it.
- Set up a fund for major purchases such as a television or car, and agree on how much you will spend on this purchase ahead of time.

- Make a special account for 'found money', such as coupon savings, bonuses, money you might have spent on cigarettes before you quit, etc. When the money accumulates, use it for something special.
- If you are anticipating a large tax refund, you may wish to have your husband change his W4 and claim less dependents so that there will be more cash on hand each payday.
- Set up a contingency fund to cover irregular expenses that crop up during the year such as weddings, funerals, car repair, etc. You may want to look over your old check registers and charge account statements to obtain a better idea of what has caught you by surprise in the past.
- Keep your budget realistic. If you constantly overspend in one category, raise it. Don't let the fact that you've strayed from your budget in one area cause you to break it in others.
- Try an automatic payroll savings plan, or include an amount for savings as part of your budget. Put aside three to six months take home pay as an emergency reserve before you leave work.
- Take advantage of specials for entertainment. Some restaurants offer two for one dinners, some theaters offer reduced prices on certain nights.
- Vacation in the off-season, and take advantage of bargain air fares or the special packages that many hotels offer.
- Avoid using credit. The interest that you must pay could be used to buy something else.
- Buy wholesale. Many companies have outlets which sell everything from jewelry to clothing at a much lower price than retail stores.
- Take advantage of free activities, such as museums, park concerts, and local festivals.
- Arrange to swap toys and clothing that your children have outgrown with friends who may have items

your children can use.
- Buy merchandise in the season it is priced lowest—air conditioners in the winter, bedsheets and linens in January, etc.
- Plant a garden and use the harvest to save on groceries.
- Visit thrift shops, second-hand shops and rummage sales for bargains.

How To Save Money On Groceries

Listed here are some tips to help you save money when you do your weekly shopping.

General Tips

- Check newspaper advertisements for the best buys, but don't travel long distances to save money' on a few items. Your transportation costs can easily wipe out any savings.
- When you shop, bring a list of the items you need— and a calculator to keep a running total.
- Experiment with generic and store brands.
- Never shop when you are hungry.
- Read labels and compare contents, price, and weight. The ingredients appear in order of proportion, with the largest first. Most labels also list nutrition information.
- Don't buy more perishable food than you will need.
- Economy size is not always cheaper. Compare prices on a per ounce basis.
- It is usually less expensive to buy in large quantities, unless the extra will go to waste.
- Plan your weekly meal menus before you shop.
- Keep a continuous shopping list in your kitchen. When you run out of an item, or think of something you'll need—jot it down.
- Try to shop only once a week.
- Use manufacturer's and store coupons.

- Buy essential foods, such as milk, eggs, bread, meat, fruit and vegetables first.
- Use refund forms. By sending in a product code, label, or box top with the manufacturer's special form, you may obtain both cash and additional coupons.
- See if your library has a coupon exchange.
- Shop in stores that give coupons a double or triple dollar value.
- Cut down on waste by apportioning the food on each plate at meal time, and eliminating serving dishes.

Bread Tips

- Buy day old bread and lunch cakes.
- Refrigerated (tube) biscuits are less expensive than biscuit mix.
- You can make your own bread crumbs from stale bread and crackers.
- Cornbread mix is less expensive than making it from scratch.

Fruit And Vegetable Tips

- Compare the price of frozen vegetables in plastic bags with the price of frozen boxed vegetables and canned vegetables. The cost per serving may be less if you purchase bags, and you can avoid waste by only using the quantity that you need for each meal.
- Buy from the bulk bins at the supermarket rather than buying pre-packaged produce. You will not only get the size, quality, and quantity that you need, but the price will generally be cheaper.
- Newspapers, radio and television stations will often report what produce is most plentiful in any given month. This information is furnished by the United States Department of Agriculture and is based on nationwide market reports. Watch for this up-to-date data on the best produce buys. These reports will also

warn of potential problems. For example: If the orange crop freezes the price of oranges will go up.

- When produce is priced by the pound, select the smaller pieces to get more servings per pound.
- Frozen fruit juices are less expensive than making the juice from fresh fruit.
- Instant mashed potatoes are less expensive than raw potatoes, and boxed potato mixes are the most expensive to buy.
- When you buy canned fruits and vegetables remember that if it has mixed pieces of various sizes it will generally cost less than cans of one style. Slices and dices are generally cheaper than whole or half styles.
- Frozen vegetables that have special sauces and seasonings are much more expensive than plain frozen vegetables.
- Often it is less expensive to buy vegetables at the end of their growing season. This is a good time to stock up and freeze your favorites.
- Buy bruised or ripe vegetables if your store sets them aside and discounts them. Use them right away.
- Buy vegetables and fruit in season.
- Compare prices—some items (such as vegetables and fruit) are cheaper when purchased frozen than when bought fresh.

Meat, Fish, And Poultry Tips

- Buy meat on sale and in larger sized cuts. Ask the butcher to cut it up, or do it yourself at home.
- When you compare foods, consider the cost per serving instead of the cost per pound. For example: 1 pound of spareribs at $ 1.89 per pound will serve one person. 1 pound of ground beef at $ 1.89 per pound will serve four people.
- Fresh turkeys are usually more expensive than frozen ones.

- Use less tender cuts of meat and marinate them, or cook them with moist heat.
- Use a meat thermometer to control shrinkage when roasting larger cuts.
- Buy bacon by the slab, it is less expensive than pre-sliced.
- Chicken breasts are usually a better buy than legs or thighs because they provide more meat per pound.
- Loin end chops are less expensive than center cut chops, but they often have as much meat.
- It is less expensive to bread your own fish filets instead of buying them already breaded.
- Fish seems expensive, but it may be a better buy on a cost per serving basis. For example: turbot has no waste.
- Pink salmon is not as expensive as red salmon.
- Grated tuna is less expensive than chunk tuna.
- Expand the amount of meat that you use by adding rice, spaghetti, noodles, or potatoes.
- If you buy lunch meat by the package, the larger packages usually cost less per ounce. Also, variety packages of lunch meats are usually more expensive than one-of-a-kind packages.
- It is cheaper to buy poultry whole and cut it up yourself.

Dairy Product Tips
- Use non-fat dry milk or evaporated milk in cooking. It is less expensive than whole milk.
- Wedges of cheese are the least expensive, and aged or sharp cheeses will cost more than processed cheese.
- Don't pay more for AA Grade eggs if you will not use them right away. AA quality will decline to grade A after one week of refrigerator storage.

A few other women share what they have learned:

Becky

"We found an interesting way to obtain new furniture—I'm not sure if anyone else will get this lucky, but it shows the advantage of keeping your eyes open. A local furniture chain had an all-night sale. They advertised that every hour a drawing would be held for $100 dollar gift certificates, and that there would be many unadvertised specials. We assumed that not too many people would be there in the pre-dawn hours, and we were right. There were about five stores within a few hours drive, so we took turns visiting each store. Since we had little competition when the drawings were held in those hours, we inevitably won the $100, or second prize of $50. We had accumulated about $400, when we began shopping. We had chosen specials in several stores that were tremendous bargains and perfect for our home. Although the chain hadn't anticipated anyone visiting several different stores in one evening we were allowed to use our accumulated gift certificates and make our purchases. With the combination of reduced prices and gift certificates, we were able to purchase $700 worth of items for only $60 of our own money! Unfortunately, the store has never had a similar sale since."

Sheila

"Our income was almost cut in half. We had to give up buying a nice car every few years, taking long vacations across the country, going out to dinner in expensive restaurants, and buying expensive clothes and gifts. Now we live with tattered furniture, and if something breaks we either fix it ourselves or wait until we can afford to pay someone else to fix it. When I was working the thought of living like this used to frighten me. Although I fantasize about having more money to spend, I like my life at home. I can watch my two year old daughter triumphantly finish a puzzle that she's been working on for an hour, or hear my son's breathless 'mom I'm home and guess what!' when he arrives from school. I can see how much my husband is able to relax and enjoy the family now that I've taken some of his responsibilities around the house. I can take the time to listen to a friend talk about her problems. I can relax and enjoy a beautiful day or just do something that I like. I know that there are no material possessions that I want badly enough to force me to go back to work.''

Barter

One way to obtain things while struggling to live on a reduced income is to try bartering. This is simply trading something you have for something you want without using money. You can try it occasionally or join a trading co-operative which supervises trades of all kinds. Check your telephone book or ask your librarian for the name of a trading club in your area.

What can be traded? There are many different items that you can consider. They include:

Skills: Business knowledge, teach something you know, foreign language ability, publicity work.

Merchandise: Unused items that you may have bought on impulse or received as gifts. Antiques or other valuables.

Handicrafts: If you have a hobby such as quilting, needle-point, painting, etc., you may be able to use your creations as a medium of exchange.

Services: Babysit, hang wallpaper, paint rooms, cook chauffer care for pets, house-sit, etc.

Before you begin bartering you should have a good idea of the value of what you are providing so that you will receive equal value in return. Your attitude towards what you have to offer can go a long way in assisting your negotiations.

Affect On Your Marriage

In addition to the many other adjustments that you are making right now, you have to deal with the changes that staying at home may have on your marriage. Without the power, security, and control of your own paycheck you will find a tremendous, if subtle change is taking place in your relationship. You are each discovering new attitudes about what you now expect from the other. Often a husband who had always treated his wife as an equal when she worked, will revert to a more traditional attitude once she stays home. In a sense, you must renegotiate the relationship that you have built your marriage on to this point. It is most important that you keep the lines of communication open during this period. Talk about your frustrations, and try to get to the root of the behavior that causes any attitudes that are disruptive. It might be that your husband was raised in a very traditional home, and feels that this is how a home with a full-time mother should be. Perhaps your own fears of dependence and wavering self-esteem are effecting your outlook and sensitivity.

Talk about the problem as often as you need to. There is no guarantee that difficulties as complicated as these can be resolved in one or two discussions. Sit down with your spouse and tell him how you feel or what you think about his attitude or actions. Don't put him on the defensive by making accusations, or put words into his mouth by telling him how he feels or thinks. Ask him for input, and try to find a common ground to begin upon. The chapter on ''Your Marriage'' provides additional suggestions for communication. Most importantly, if one way doesn't work, don't give up. Think of another way, and another way after that, until you have found a solution that works for both of you.

One of the biggest problems you may face with your husband is his resentment towards your not working. It doesn't matter if he encouraged you to leave, or how much he enjoys the extra time and attention that you now have for him, there are going to be periods when he is overwhelmed with the responsibility of being the sole breadwinner. A few other women explain:

Marlene

"My husband had to take on a second job. Although we had both agreed that I should stay home with the baby, it didn't stop the feelings of guilt that I had when I watched him hurry from one job to the other. When our clothes washer and television stopped working in the same week, he became very upset. He was depressed, worried, and extremely anxious about our finances. Then he started criticizing. 'I wasn't working because I was lazy.' 'I had talked him into staying at home.' 'I had a lackadaisical attitude toward money.' I tried to be understanding, but I was spending my days with a cranky baby, and I wasn't going to put up with his constant critical commentary. I was angry, but I managed to stay calm. I pointed out that my returning to work would mean that we must buy a new car (more payments), pay a babysitter, eat out more often and buy new clothes (I hadn't reached my old weight yet). I wasn't sure if my income could cover all of those expenses and still justify me working. We sat down and calculated everything, then discovered that we would only end up about $300 a month ahead (until the car was paid off in three years). Then we each made a list of the pros and cons of my staying at home. We were both astonished when his list of pros' turned out to be twice as long as mine! It helped us to reinforce our initial belief that the decision for me to stay home would be best for us as a family. Because it was so glaringly obvious how he truly felt, I became more confident in my role and he was finally more supportive."

Valerie

"We seldom argued about spending before I stopped working. Now, it seems like that is our main form of communication. I knew I would have to change my buying habits when I left my job, and I think I have managed fairly well. But my husband just buys himself or the family whatever he wants. He'll come home with tickets to a baseball game (and a family spending a day at the ballpark isn't cheap), or announce that we are visiting an expensive amusement park without discussing it with me beforehand. Naturally once the children are all excited, I'm the ogre if I refuse to go along. Or he'll buy things that we don't need—a new portable television (we have three) or a home computer (it's still in the closet). His attitude is 'I have all this pressure, so I deserve to have whatever makes me happy'. Not only is it childish, but we can't afford it. "

As a homemaker your worth is based on human instead of monetary contributions. Your being at home enriches the lives of your family, but you seldom receive any tangible appreciation for your efforts. We each need a degree of independence and control in our lives, and every home-maker needs some money of her own to continue that feeling. You may find that the dependence that you feel without funds of your own affects your feelings of self-worth, and your confidence in your ability to remain an equal partner in your marriage. A few women discuss the frustrations they have encountered:

Charlotte

"I never wanted to feel completely dependent, so I set aside money of my own before I stopped working. A few months after I quit we had a tremendous financial setback. Due to a shakeup at my husband's company, his salary was reduced and he lost some of his benefits. Around the same time our daughter became seriously ill and required constant medical attention. Between the cut in income and the large medical expenses, I ended up using my savings to pay the bills. After it was gone, and my daughter had improved, I was left without my security. I felt frustrated and vulnerable. I didn't want to resume my career—my close call with Nancy made me value the time I had with her even more. Yet I couldn't stand the idea of not having my own money and the independence it gave me. Luckily, I have always enjoyed embroidery and quilting. I began making items and selling them at local craft fairs. It doesn't make me rich, but now I have some money that I can call my own."

Ruth

"When I stopped working my husband was afraid I wouldn't be able to stay within our budget. He wanted me to account for every expense, and justify every purchase. Naturally, it drove me crazy. Our relationship was getting more and more strained, and I seriously considered returning to work. Instead, I sat down with him and went over the budget. We broke down every expense that wasn't fixed, such as groceries, home improvements, etc., and I gave him a realistic idea of what the expenses would be. We set up funds for each area, and used a small amount of his paycheck each week to support them. For example, we set aside $20 a week towards possible appliance or home repairs, $15 each week for potential medical expenses (doctor visits, prescriptions, etc.), and $20 a week for family entertainment. Then we alloted an allowance for each of us ($30 a week) for personal expenses such as clothes, gifts, and whatever else we wanted to buy. That thirty dollars does not have to be accounted for, everything else does. This method is much easier to live with. We needed more control over our finances, but we also needed money of our own."

Deborah

"My husband received a promotion and a healthy raise. We decided that it would be a good time for me to stop working and stay home with the children, because we could now make it without my salary. Still, I hesitated at the loss of having my own money, so we compromised. By cutting back a few of our expenses, we decided that a portion of that raise could be my money. We selected the amount by computing how much of the increase would be needed to offset my income (after babysitters and other work related expenses), how much would be needed to sustain his new position (entertaining, etc.), and how much would be needed for taxes. The amount left was mine, and went into my personal checking account every pay-day—to spend or save as I pleased. There are times when I use it to buy extras for the house, or treat the family to some adventure. But it's important that I have the freedom to spend it where and when I please."

Lucy

"My husband balked at the idea of giving me money of my own. 'If you want something, you know I would give you the money' he'd say. That obviously wasn't the point. I didn't want to ask for it, or have to discuss every purchase with him. I felt that I was contributing to the welfare of the family, and that it should be valued. To pay someone else to care for the children, clean the house, and make the meals was way beyond our means without my salary. Yet I was doing it all. I knew that there wasn't a lot of money to spare in our budget, but after examining it carefully it seemed like $50 a week would not harm us too badly. I sat down and had a talk with him, and tried to stress how important having the independence of some money of my own was to me. It didn't sink in. First he accused me of trying to use the money as a fund to leave him. When we settled that, he wanted to know exactly what I planned to do with the money. I stressed again that the whole point was the freedom it would give me to buy what I pleased—whether it was clothes, something for the house, or whatever. He still didn't like it, but I stood my ground. After several weeks, he finally agreed. Now he'll lay on the guilt every once in awhile, mentioning some nice thing we could do or buy with 'all that money he gives me'. I resent it, but I ignore it. I know I deserve my own money, and if he's unhappy, that's his problem. There's no guarantee in life that you are going to be happy all the time anyway.''

Handling Your Money

With the change from career to homemaker will come a corresponding change in the way you handle your finances. You will probably have to work harder to stretch your income, and there are times when you will disagree on how it should be spent. There may be clashes in values (a vacation or new furniture?), or struggles for control (should we save this bonus or splurge on something for the family?). It was easier to ignore conflicts when you both had a paycheck coming in. There was more money to work with, and your income gave you additional clout. It may help to take a few moments and examine your attitude about money. Once you understand the basis of some of your feelings and reactions, you may find it easier to communicate them to your spouse, and work out a compromise when necessary.

What does money mean to you? Is it a source of self-esteem? A means of power? A way to accumulate the many things you desire? Something that allows you to make a better life for your children? The freedom to spend as you please—when you please? For most of us, it means a little bit of all of these things. The best way to find out what you value the most is to imagine that you have inherited several million dollars. What would you do with the money? Let's say that you would buy a fabulous mansion. What pleasures do you anticipate from that purchase? Do you fantasize how impressed your friends would be? Or how wonderful you would look walking through it? Do you believe that it would open doors for you socially? The point of course, is your expectations. You can be disappointed at times when your expectations have been met. For example, instead of being impressed by your mansion, your friends may feel uncomfortable in it or jealous, and drift away. There's never a guarantee that getting something that you want in life will generate the feelings and rewards that you had hoped for.

With a clearer idea of your attitude and values, take a moment and compare them with those of your husband. Do you share the same goals? How would he have spent the millions? If your goals conflict a great deal, you may have discovered the hidden source of your current disagreements. All couples argue about finances at times, and they may range from a low key comment to long-running battles. The most common areas are:

- One accuses the other of spending too much.
- One accuses the other of being too stingy.
- One wants complete control of the finances.
- One wants to live beyond the current income.
- One disagrees with overall spending goals.

In addition, your individual personalities have a major influence on your attitudes. If you are a worrier, and your husband is philosophical; or if you enjoy taking risks while your husband is conservative, there are bound to be conflicts about how your money is spent. The only way to work through these problems is to talk it, and find a workable balance. You may have to begin by finding a small patch of common ground that you both agree on, and building from there. In other instances, you may find alternatives that will meet both of your needs, or find that a little give and take is necessary.

How important are material things? We obviously like them, but at times it may seem that we over-value them. I'm not talking about what we consider basics (two televisions and two cars for every family), but about our national obsession to continually upgrade what we have, buying bigger, more improved cars and televisions as often as we can. We also have a compulsion to be the first, or one of the first, to pick up the latest 'must have' item, whether it's a home computer, V.C.R., food processor, or a robot.

When you allow yourselves to define your needs by what your neighbors have, or by what advertisers and news articles trumpet as the new 'in' thing, you will never be satisfied. There will always be something that you feel deprived of, and something that you are craving. In addition, you are passing these attitudes on to your children—although you seldom notice unless it's Christmas and there are none of the latest 'must have' items left in stock at any toy store on the continent. (You know because you looked).

You can slowly turn away from these attitudes if you learn to ignore the call to buy, and place more value on the things that cannot be bought. It also doesn't hurt to spend some time considering the real cost of everything that you own. Your lamps, your video cassette recorder, your clothing, etc., are all investments that you have made. You have paid good money to obtain an item that you hope will yield you something in return. Are you receiving a good return on your investment for the items you own? Are the yields worth the price that you have paid? How many things have you bought in the last year that are already buried in a closet or attic? Every item that you own takes time. You must pay for it, carry it home, find a place to put it, care for it, protect it, and when you tire of it—find a way to get rid of it—or a place to store it. How many things are really worth all of that trouble?

What are your real needs? What can you live without? Sometimes it's surprising how much can be left in the stores if you develop the right attitude towards buying. One tactic is to delay a purchase for awhile. Something that seems essential today may seem less important in two weeks, and unnecessary in a month. Try practicing this tactic whenever possible.

There is nothing wrong with spending money to purchase things that give you, or your family pleasure. The idea is to maximize the pleasure that you can obtain with the money that you have. If you save money by re-upholstering a chair instead of buying a new one, you may be able to use the funds for a family outing, or a weekend getaway. Decide what your priorities are, what you value the most, and what will allow you the greatest enjoyment over time, then concentrate your finances in those areas.

A Salary For Wives?

Every once in awhile we homemakers can comfort ourselves with the latest survey. Some research department at a major university announces that the value of a homemaker's worth is now $7 or $8 dollars an hour. We fantasize about how nice it would be to have such a tangible reward for our efforts, and how we would spend the money if we had it. However, there isn't a very good chance that a paycheck is coming to you soon. You see, no one can decide where to get the money from. Unless your family is well-to-do, it's unlikely that your husband can afford to pay you. Your old employer isn't likely to take up the cause and keep you on the payroll. The government, with its soaring deficits and continual program cuts isn't a very good source either (although that is where most people place their hopes). Our money is what keeps the government going, and without enough to go around as it is, such an enormous program would require either a tremendous tax increase, or a devaluation of the dollar. Neither seems like a workable alternative, because although you would have a paycheck, you would still have the same money problems that you now have without it.

When You Need More Money

There may be times that you have no choice, you must generate some type of income to ease the financial pressure. It may not be practical to return to your career, and you are looking for other ways to bring in extra cash. The chapter on. "Expanding Interests" provides a few suggestions.

SECTION FOUR

Where To Begin

What About You?

Your self-image is influenced by the different roles and relationships in your life. You are already someone's wife, daughter, sister, neighbor, mother, and friend. You may also be an avid reader, tennis player, gardener, pianist, or patron of the arts. Each quality brings out different aspects of your personality. However, the role that may have had the greatest impact on your feelings of self-worth was that of a career woman. You may not have recognized its significance until after you stopped working, but once you are left without the continual esteem of your peers and the tangible rewards of a job, you may find yourself struggling with your identity. One woman explains:

"I stared in the mirror for a long time on my 35th birthday. There were plenty of laugh crinkles around my eyes, and grey was sprinkled throughout my hair. I couldn't remember what it felt like to be 25. I found myself wondering—who is this person? She used to be the manager of an office with a responsibility for several million dollars in receivables and 8 employees. She used to make witty remarks that made intelligent people laugh and enjoy her company. Now, all that I could see in the reflection was Sandy's mother and Dave's wife.

When I left my career I promised myself that I wouldn't change, that my identity would remain strong—but somehow it still managed to slip away when I wasn't looking. Somewhere along the dishes, and the laundry, and listening to my family's daily problems, I forgot to make time for me. But home-making is also a hazardous career The dangers aren't as obvious as working as a trapeze artist, but they are there just the same, With any other job you receive some type of acknowledgement or reward when you do it well. As a homemaker, I'm expected to have bright and healthy kids, a happy husband, a clean home, and delightful meals. My motivation is supposed to be love, and I should be satisfied with the privilege of having time for myself as a reward. As a person who tries to excel at everything that she does, this only made me work harder. Somehow I felt that if I could only do it better and faster, the esteem would magically appear. Instead, I became the stereotypical housewife, lost in her family and their concerns, worried over trivial details, and with few personal interests or activities. Because I stopped being aware of my identity, I didn't notice when it started to disappear.

I've changed since that birthday. It's been a long slow and sometimes painful process, but I managed to change what I could and make peace with the rest. Today, I am still Dave's wife and Sandy's mother, but I am also a person who pursues hopes and dreams and deserves time and attention. I've rediscovered a friend that I don't want to lose again."

It's time to reaffirm who you are, and how you are projecting yourself in your new lifestyle. You want to insure that your inner identity is firm, so that your feelings of self-worth are not overly influenced by the attitudes and opinions of other people. If you allow that kind of dependence into your life, you may find yourself buffeted by too many influences, left at the mercy of criticisms and opinions of others, and disappointed when you do not receive the support that you expect from other people. You may learn that those you are striving to please are too busy with their own lives, unwilling or unable to express what you need, or uncaring about your needs. Once you discover how to find satisfaction through yourself, you will be more secure about your role, and more happy with your life.

How are you responding to the attitudes of other people toward your new lifestyle? Do you often feel angry or frustrated, as if you must justify your existence? Are you anxious to prove them wrong? A few other women share their viewpoints:

Janet

"It's an odd feeling when you are treated as a curiosity. I remember one woman I met at a charity fund raiser. She automatically assumed that I was a fellow business woman, and she seemed to enjoy confiding in me. She gave a detailed description of her plans to get ahead, shared her opinion of different management styles, and told me that she had no plans to marry, because a husband or children would only get in the way. I hadn't said five words, until she finally asked 'and what do you do?' I was tempted to lie and simply match her story with tales of the career I left—merely pretend that I had never stopped working. Instead I told her that I was a homemaker. She was speechless. 'I thought your type went out with peddle-pushers' she said. I started to give an angry response, but then I thought, 'this poor woman doesn't know anything about the benefits of personal relationships, I'll try and help her to understand'. So I began describing the pleasure I receive from pursuing my own interests at home, the wonders of married life and the joys of children—until I looked at her eyes and realized that she wasn't capable of understanding. I gave up. She would never stop thinking of me as someone who lacked in drive and ambition, or be able to comprehend my decision to leave my career. Later, I decided that if I met someone who is interested in my lifestyle because they have considered trying it, then it's worth discussing. Otherwise, it's pointless—they will never understand.''

Bonnie

"My initial response to someone who treated me as a dizzy housewife was very childish. I was cornered by a smart-aleck at a party, who subjected me to a tedious monologue on how a woman's place is in the home, and how they are unfit for any positions of power and authority. I verbally toyed with him until he turned his ignorance loose on the economy. Since I had been an economist, I threw out an intricate and complicated monetarist theory and asked for his opinion. While he stumbled around for an answer, I walked away.

Today, I don't allow such attitudes to bother me. If I meet or must spend time with someone who insults me, I don't argue or fight back. Instead, I refuse to acknowledge their prejudicial opinions. In most cases, the person will either walk away to search out another potential victim, or readjust their perception of me. It forces them to see me as a person, not as a symbol.''

Pamela

"Non-conformists seem to run in my family. During the 1960's, when the traditional housewife was still the norm, my mother was a busy executive. She struggled with other people's opinions and attitudes for years, before it finally became fashionable to work and have children. Here in the 1980's, while everyone that I know has a career, I enjoy staying at home. I believe that this lifestyle is the best one for me, and unlike my mother, I ignore the criticism. If someone says 'How could you throw your chances for a career away—don't you care about yourself?' I tell them that it was a conscious decision, and the best possible one for me. The fact that I don't fit the popular mold is not my problem. I expect them to respect my choice, just as I respect theirs. I think that that expectation has made a big difference in the way that I am treated. Because I am so comfortable and assured of my decision, I seldom see or hear any adverse comments.''

What Do You Call Yourself?

Being asked "What do you do?" for the first time can be an unnerving experience. Until that moment, housewives or homemakers were always other women. You resist accepting those labels because you don't feel that those words can really explain who you are, and you fear that using them will lock you into any attitudes or stereotypes that come with the role. You search for another word or definition that will portray what you are and do, but grant you more recognition and acceptance.

Other women have tried that—calling themselves 'leisure persons', 'household engineers', 'family co-ordinators', environment formulators', and 'home supervisors'. What they have discovered is that the name doesn't matter, if is the attitude towards the role that generates the problem. A different word to describe your new job will not change the attitude of people who are prejudiced. What you must learn to do is to move beyond any anger or frustration you feel towards such bias, and examine the real question that they are asking.

If someone asks "What do you do?", there's a good chance that they don't know you, or haven't seen you for some time. While it's true that some people ask that question so that they can slap a label on you, then impress you with their superiority; many others are really asking "What kind of person are you?" "Do we have interests in common?" You can find many ways to answer those real questions, without creating new labels for yourself. Remember, you are the same wonderful, loveable, exciting person that you were when you had a career. Once you rediscover your strengths, potentials, and values, you can easily command the respect and attention of others by using your abilities.

Your Identity

Do you have a positive image of your inner self, the person that you really are? No matter how successful and assured you appear on the outside, there are often doubts on the inside. If you are like most people, you are often disappointed in yourself, and are your own sternest critic. The key to a strong self-image begins with that private part of yourself, the one that daydreams, plans, and travels with you through all of your other roles. Take the time to define and examine who you are today—you may be surprised to discover qualities that you are currently unaware of. Most of the questions here are ones you might ask any potential friend whom you wanted to learn more about. They begin very simply, and become progressively more complicated.

- What is your favorite color?
- What is your favorite food?
- What is your favorite style of furniture?
- What is your favorite car?
- What is your favorite clothing style?
- What is your favorite season of the year?
- What is your favorite song?
- What is your favorite book?
- What is your favorite movie?
- What is your favorite television program?
- What is your favorite sport?

- Do you prefer the city or the country?
- Are you a day or a night person?
- What is your favorite restaurant?
- Where is your favorite vacation spot?
- What is your dream vacation?
- Who do you admire the most?

- Who is your best friend?
- What political party do you usually agree with?
- What section of the newspaper do you read first?
- What is your least favorite chore?

- What do you value the most in life?
- Do you believe in God?
- Can you explain your religious beliefs?
- What frightens you the most?
- What makes you the happiest?
- Do you usually trust people?
- Do you prefer company or solitude?
- Do you enjoy doing things for others?
- Are you easily bored?
- What has been your most embarrassing moment?
- What has been your most triumphant moment?
- What motivates you?

- Can you tolerate criticism?
- Do you like to try new things?
- Do you prefer physical or mental activities?
- Do you prefer your family to friends? (Or vice versa?)
- Are you a worrier?
- Do you become concerned about what other people think?
- How do you respond to anger projected at you?
- Do you tend to keep your thoughts to yourself?
- Do you listen more than you talk?
- Do you keep your promises?

- Can you admit your mistakes?
- Can you express your feelings?
- Can you ask for your needs to be met?
- Do you generally feel good about yourself?
- Do you have many friends?
- How do you spend your spare time?
- What habits and hobbies have you had since

childhood?
- Do you prefer a placid, well-ordered life?
- Do you feel comfortable being yourself?
- How often do you project your best self?

Once you have responded to these questions, ask your husband or a friend to guess what you answered. By comparing their impressions to your own, you can begin to recognize any difference between the way that you perceive yourself and the way that others see you.

Then take a break. Are you learning anything? Do you feel uncomfortable or unsure about some of your answers? The next exercise is a little more fun:

Pretend that you are a detective or an archeologist looking for clues, trying to recreate a description of yourself. Begin by examining the contents of your purse. What do they say about you? Then do the same thing with your house and the rest of your belongings. How would a stranger describe you based on what he saw? How does your conclusion make you feel about yourself?

Now it's time to delve a little deeper. Finish the following sentences as quickly as possible:

- I like . . .
- I dislike . . .
- It makes me angry that . . .
- I am proud that I . . .
- I am looking forward to . . .
- I wish . . .
- I like people who . . .
- My friends don't know that . . .
- I know that I can . . .
- I would like my husband to . . .
- People look up to me because . . .
- I am a person who never . . .
- You can count on me to . . .
- I'm often misunderstood when . . .

- Other people see me as . . .
- What I really want is to be . . .

What kind of changes have you made in your life so far? To help identify them—try this:

Think of an old friend that you haven't seen in about ten years. Imagine that you have bumped into each other, and after a few hours of exchanging news, you begin to really talk. What can you tell them about the changes in yourself over the last ten years?

ASK YOURSELF:
- If all possibilities were open to you, what would you do first?
- What do you think of regularly before you fall asleep?
- If you could be anyone in the world, who would it be?
- How would you like to be married to you?
- How would you like to be your friend?

Some of these questions will require a great deal of thought, and may be difficult to answer at first. But they will provide an overall portrait of who you are, and who you would like to be. You may discover that you haven't spent enough time thinking about yourself lately—that you know the answers that your husband or a friend would give, but not your own. Or you may discern that you are not always the person that you thought you were. What is important is that you have begun to discover yourself, and once you know who you are, you can make any changes that you like. Just as you became the person that you are today, you can make changes to create the person that you would like to be.

How do you feel about yourself? For a homemaker to survive in a frustrating minority that is often put down or made to feel inferior, she must nurture her self-confidence, pride, and independence. In addition, strong feelings of self-worth are necessary to provide her with the strength to face adversity in her life, and allow her the courage to grow.

How Do You Feel About Yourself?

Here are some additional questions to consider:

- Would you say that you love yourself?
- How well can you accept the person that you are?
- Are you afraid that others will discover the 'real' you and reject you?
- Would you rather be somebody else? Why?
- Do you need your choices validated by the approval of others?
- Do you have difficulty accepting compliments?
- Do you feel guilty when you indulge in a selfish activity?
- Do you take good care of yourself?
- Can you pinpoint the source of whatever negative feelings you have toward yourself?

The answers that reflect the strongest self-esteem are obvious. No matter how well we have succeeded in other portions of our lives, as women we often sacrifice attention to our inner self for other concerns. Yet if you can recognize your behavior and its origin, you can work to change your responses. And if you can change your responses, you will improve your feelings about yourself.

Building Self-Esteem

Draw up a list of your positive traits. It doesn't matter if there are two items or twenty, they provide a place to begin. If you remind yourself regularly of your better qualities, you can increase your awareness of them and feel better about yourself. That in turn may heighten your awareness of other favorable characteristics you possess, which can be further developed through positive reinforcement.

One way to begin is to concentrate on strengths that you had exhibited in your career. A little imagination can help you to see any applications they may have in your home life. In addition, a reminder of yourself as a strong and confident woman can help to bolster your ego as a homemaker. Try to act the same way that you did when you were working— walk, talk, look, think, and portray confidence in everything that you do.

Your friends can also influence your outlook. If they are often negative, it will be harder for you to avoid depression. I'm not saying that you should drop your less cheerful friends, but try to spend extra time with the confident and upbeat ones. Because there are few role models for homemakers today, you must draw on several sources. One solution is to adopt a role model that helped you in your career to your life as a homemaker. Here is an example:

Carolyn

"Most of us learned to psyche ourselves up and project a certain image in our careers. It helped us to get through difficult situations, and to be treated more professionally by sceptics. For example, I worked with a man who really knew how to project an image. He not only dressed for success, he exuded success. I learned a lot from him. You could almost watch him wrap himself up in an aura, and he would walk, talk, and look like a person of importance. He was always treated that way too. The most important people in the room would always drift his way, and his peers always held him in awe. You may not think of doing the same thing as a homemaker, but you should. If someone is putting me down for being a homemaker, or I just feel like a drab nonentity, I find myself thinking of him. I try to bring back that feeling of power, and project it. It really helps."

A few other women share how they became more confident:

Judy

"I used to be terrified of animals. Whenever I visited friends who had pets, especially dogs, I would insist that they put them in another room. It's impossible for someone who hasn't had similar fears to understand the irrational terror that you feel. I was sure that the dog would find some way to hurt me if it had half a chance. If a dog barked, I always assumed that it was a prelude to something worse. Now we have a dog! On impulse during a weak moment, I bought one as a gift for my husband who had been wanting one for some time. It was a small puppy (they never frightened me as much as grown dogs). I assumed that my best chance for having a pet that didn't harm me was to start out with one when it was very young. I hoped that I could eradicate my fears as the puppy grew. I have to say that I had no idea of the time and responsibility having a pet means when I bought it, but we've been fortunate because we have a very smart, well-behaved dog. Now, I'm not frightened at all. The day to day companionship the dog has given us has been more enjoyable than I ever imagined. In fact, I'm as attached to her as my husband is. But the remarkable thing about overcoming my fear is that it has changed my attitude about so many things. Not only am I more comfortable around other animals, I have more courage to take risks, and to try new things. I feel better about myself because I overcame this phobia, and I know now that if I could conquer this tremendous fear, I can vanquish a lot of other obstacles too."

Jill

"We all want to improve ourselves, but making the effort isn't always easy. I used to buy self-help books and tapes, promising myself a new beginning as soon as I got a chance to read or listen to them. Instead they sat on my shelf—the time was never right. One day, in sheer boredom I picked one up. It was almost silly in some ways, but when I finished it I felt better about myself. I began to make it a habit, whenever things got me down, to read or listen to one of them. I have found that over time, different ideas have sunk in, and I've slowly begun to feel much better about myself. The most important thing that I've learned is that who you are begins within you—that all the fame and fortune in the world will not matter enough if you don't like yourself.''

With a strong self image you are better able to cope with stress, less likely to become depressed, and more apt to succeed in your goals. Here is what other women have discovered:

Cathy

''I had a difficult time making the adjustment to staying at home. I became very depressed and nervous, and although I was unhappy, I knew I didn't want to return to work. My husband never wanted me to quit, and instead of listening to my concerns he made it a daily campaign for me to return to my job. It must have been my pride, or my stubborn streak, but I didn't want to admit that my friends were right when they said that I would be back to work in six months. My depression seemed to feed on itself. I felt like I was nothing, and that no one appreciated me. I was anxious, irritable, and I worried constantly about our finances. I was terribly lonely. I don't know how I finally snapped out of it, but somewhere in there I began to examine who I was and where I was going. I didn't like what I saw. Now the popular alternative is to go back to work to solve these kinds of problems, but I decided to try it another way I practically forced myself to take a long walk every day. The exercise cleared my head, and I seemed to be able to think better away from the house.

I was able to pay attention to nature for the first time in ages, really looking at the sky, the trees, the flowers. It was amazing to realize how these little worlds are continually going on while we are all wrapped up in our careers and homes. I became fascinated by the many birds that I would see in my walks, and soon I was bringing along a book to identify them and a pair of binoculars. I became an enthusiastic, but very amateur bird watcher. It helped me to break the monotony, and the feelings that frustrated me so. Of course that one interest didn't replace the excitement of a career, but soon I was starting other projects, and making plans for the future. My confidence grew, and I could see myself in this life at home. My husband started to enjoy having me there, to listen to him without being distracted by my own job or problems, and to have a nice homey atmosphere for him to come home to. I really became a more exciting person. I found new interests to intrigue me, and had time to think about things, form opinions and develop ideas that were not work-oriented. I'm incredibly glad that I didn't take the easy way out and go back to work, because I love my life now.''

Debbie

''I was sure that I was the only one who didn't have it all together. If I saw a woman walking down the street, striding purposefully with her briefcase, I was sure that she was successful and loved it—probably never had the doubts that I did. If I watched a woman play in the park with her children, I was sure that she was the ultimate mother, and never had a second thought about the life she could be having in the workforce. Everyone else seemed so confident and assured of what they were doing, and what they wanted. Sometimes I thought I knew. I would set goals and reach them, but nothing was ever enough to completely satisfy me. Finally I decided to resign my position, and take some time at home to re-evaluate my life. Of course, I used my children need me' as an excuse. Before I left, I was surprised by the number of my co-workers who confided that they secretly thought about leaving, but wouldn't or couldn't take the step. I realized that no one is as sure about themselves as I assumed they were, and that understanding made my decision easier. Once I stayed home, I had more time to think about myself, to grow and to cultivate relationships. I developed new interests and confidence in my abilities. My new perspective made me more assured about my decision. Now, everyone seems to view me as 'the one who has it all together'!''

The key to self-esteem is finding a balance between the control that you have over your life and your fears. Without a balance, you may find your energies scattered in many different directions, fizzling away without any real purpose. Women who are happy staying at home usually feel competent with their lifestyle, confident of their decision, and are able to see a potential for future happiness.

It is important that you have a part of your life where you can achieve and accomplish something, and a part that gives you satisfaction and pleasure. For example, your husband or children may meet the second requirement, your job or outside interests the first. If your life is filled with accomplishments, but few intimate relationships—it will be out of balance (and vice versa). Because a homemaker receives so little appreciation or reward for her work, it is essential that she create such a balance on her own.

By recognizing the need for a well-rounded life, and trusting yourself to fulfill it, you can become the person that you were meant (or would like) to be. With the strength you had as a career woman, the control you have in your life, your ability to be flexible, and a strong inner rooted identity, you no longer have to prove anything to the outside world.

You will value and respect your own needs, and help others to do the same. With support, encouragement, and love from others and for yourself, you can claim your own life and live it to the fullest.

Life Planning

During your career you made straightforward plans for your success. They gave you an unswerving purpose as you overcame obstacles and targeted your objectives. To maintain control and direction in your new lifestyle as a homemaker, you must continue to formulate specific goals. Your plans should reflect your needs for personal happiness and growth as a homemaker.

The stereotypical problems of housewives are usually a result of poor planning and vague ambitions. With unlimited freedom and no game plan it is easy to become bored, lonely, and dependent upon other people for your happiness. Or you may find that you have allowed the demands of others to infringe upon your time, and that you are so heavily overscheduled that you have simply traded old pressures and problems for new ones.

At first, you have so many ideas for using your time at home that goals will seem unneccessary. You have household chores crying for attention; paperwork that needs to be organized; letters you have been meaning to write; visits you have been planning to make; books you have wanted to read; and activities with your husband and children that you have been looking forward to doing. However, this flurry of activity will gradually cease, and some projects will lose their appeal. When this happens, it is time to create new aspirations.

It will not be easy for you to set straightforward goals. The needs of your family may sometimes conflict with your own hopes and dreams, and at times you must make painful sacrifices to accomplish what you really want. Begin with small ambitions and build from your success. If you set goals that are too large they can easily overwhelm you. In addition, you may be ambivalent about your plans. Perhaps you are unsure how long you will remain a homemaker, or how and if you will resume your career. With few contemporary role models to guide you, your ambitions must be the ones that you create.

Setting Goals

In order to have a clear picture of what goals to strive for, you must thoroughly examine your life and your needs. Begin by writing a summary of your life, as if you were telling your story to a stranger who knows nothing about you. Don't edit or limit what you write because it is for your eyes only. Then read it over. Has your life followed the direction you had anticipated? Have you achieved your goals in the past? Examine it objectively. What does this person need to make her life a better one? Now, write out a new story. This time the subject will be "If you could live your life over again, how would you do it?".

These exercises should give you a better overall picture of the course you would like to pursue. The following questions will help you to obtain some specific ideas for your strategy:

- Is there anything that you have always wanted to try but have never had the time or courage?
- How are your happiest moments spent?
- What would you like to spend more time doing?
- What do you daydream about? (They are often goals in a formative stage.)
- If you received $100,000 tommorrow, how would you spend it?
- What could happen in your life to make it a better one?

- What do you want to accomplish at this point in your life?
- Imagine yourself retired and looking over your past, what would you have liked your life to include?

Here is a list of elements in your personal life to set goals for. Each should have a series of goals, such as: three months, one year, five years, ten years. Write down what you would like to have happen in each of those areas. Writing it will help to implant the ideas more firmly in your mind. Set personal goals for the following aspects:

Marriage	Children	Health
Lifestyle	Intellect	Social
Home	Community	Spiritual
Family	Professional	Financial
Physical	Material	Friendship

Examine your intentions. What can you do to make them happen? What are your priorities? Are you moving toward them or away from them? Now, develop a plan of action by organizing your time and resources to achieve what you desire. Your strategies should match your needs, physically, mentally, and spiritually. If you set traps for yourself by outlining what you feel you should do, or are *expected* to do, you won't accomplish your goals.

A friend who used these ideas was willing to share the goals that she set for herself. For some of you, they may seem too idealistic, for others—not challenging enough. While reading through her thoughts, compare them with your own hopes and expectations of the future.

Physical
3 months: Be more aware of my eating habits. Start a regular exercise program.

1 year: Continue to exercise regularly. Lose 15 lbs. Begin to participate in a physical activity—maybe

swimming—as often as possible.

5 years: Have myself, and the rest of my family in good physical shape with regular physical exercise and good dietary habits.

10 years: Physical fitness is now a second nature to all of us. We look good and are in good health.

Intellect

3 months: Bring myself up-to-date on current events. Read more challenging books.

1 year: Attend lectures and seminars on topics of interest. Join or start a discussion group.

5 years: Sign up at the university for courses that I am interested in. Become more active in speaking out for issues that I feel strongly about.

10 years: Continually find new challenges and keep myself interesting and stimulated. Pass these attitudes and values on to my children.

Spiritual

3 months: Attend church, pray, read the bible more often. Cultivate more friendships through church.

1 year: Become more active in church activities, especially in helping others. Take part in a retreat/renewal program.

5 years: Teach bible school and lead prayer meetings. Begin programs for elderly and handicapped that are needed but not currently available.

10 years: Be a living example of my beliefs, and help others in their spiritual development.

Home

3 months: Become more adjusted to staying at home. Re-organize housekeeping routine and do a complete cleaning.

1 year: Make more of an effort to create a home environment that both our family and friends enjoy.

Repaint rooms, start planting flowers. Create an area where I can work on my craft projects undisturbed.

5 years: Have my dream flower garden completed. Entertain often.

10 years: Have downstairs rooms completely redecorated, sponsor a foreign exchange student.

There are five elements necessary for succeeding in your endeavors. They are:

Find a balance. When something is obstructing your goals try to find a way around it, or a way to integrate it with the rest of your life.

Set a clear direction. Unless you clarify what you want, it would be difficult to follow a course to your objectives.

Create short term goals that reflect your long term needs. Because your sense of purpose will often be frustrated, work toward your target one step at a time.

Understand that no single goal holds the key to your happiness. Some of our dreams will be more important than others. But obtaining one particular aspiration will not be enough to make your life a perfect one.

Know your priorities. Pinpoint the things that are most important to you, so that you can concentrate your energies on them.

By having a clear idea of what you want and what you must do to obtain it, reaching your goals becomes a simple matter of following the plan that you outline, and persevering until you complete it. Yet sometimes you can obtain what you wish for, but in a different way than you had planned. Here is an example:

Ann
"I spent a great deal of time deciding what I wanted to do, and to my surprise I concluded that I would like

to write. It had always been something I thought about in the back of my mind, but I had never seriously considered it as a goal in my life. Once I was sure that this was what I wanted to do, I made a plan. My goal was to have several short stories published, and be well into my first novel at the end of four years. Through twists and turns of fate, I have never had a chance to submit any fictional work. But I have had three non-fiction books published. I exceeded my goal, but in a way that I had never expected!''

Another woman is working toward her goals in a different manner:

Julie

''It started as an idea. I was a new mother then, and I kept thinking, why doesn't somebody make a better baby dish? The thought of trying to create and market one myself was a bit overwhelming—I still hadn't gotten used to being a mother, or staying at home! I wasn't even sure if I wanted to have my own business.

One day while I was shopping I picked up some odds and ends and went home and created a prototype. It tried it out, and it worked. The excitement and pride that I felt was enough to encourage me further. I knew absolutely nothing about creating and marketing a product, but I decided that I could learn. I managed to squeeze in one hour a week at the library. For weeks I poured over books and magazines, taking notes. Then I made a plan. I don't have a lot of time or money to devote to it, but I found that if I do it in small steps, I can handle it.

I have lined up three companies to show the product to, and a place to produce it. I don't want to get overly involved in this, but it has exciting possibilities. And now that I know how to go about it, I have several other ideas that I would like to try and develop.''

You deserve to make the best possible life for yourself, and by continuing to strive for new achievements, you will never stop being the personally satisfied woman that you want to be.

Expanding Interests

No matter if you are homebound, financially strapped, or subjected to a demanding family, it is extremely important that you continue to develop new outside interests in your life. They will help you to remain a stimulating and independent person. Your body, mind and spirit will weaken if they are neglected, and frustration, depression, restlessness and illness can result. Retaining outside contacts and interests is not a luxury, it is essential to your physical and mental health.

Without enough activities to invigorate you, even the most enlightened woman can become overly dependent on her husband and children by trying to live her life through them. And yet, it is easy to avoid recognizing this trap. You might insist "I don't have the time", "I don't have anyone that I want to spend the time with", "I don't have anything that I want to talk about", or "I don't need other people to entertain me".

Although some women need less social contact than others, we all require a certain degree of companionship and entertainment. If this wasn't the case, why would prisoners be punished by being placed in isolation? In addition to contact with others, we all need interests that will expand our abilities and provide us with outlets for our energy.

Homemakers who are happy with their lives have a-chieved some measure of balance and control. A life dedicated to others cannot be a balanced one. Time dictated by the needs of others is not controlled. Instead of asking yourself "Should I take on additional interests?", you should be deciding what you will do, where you will do it, and when you will begin.

During your busy career you may have fantasized about the freedom of staying at home. Yet the most obvious part of that freedom is the ability to select your own activities, and to create a schedule that is most satisfying to you. You have the prerogative to choose what parts of your life you would like to enhance at this point, and in what ways you would like to fill your time.

Balancing your interests with the rest of your life requires planning. If you choose activities that are suited to you, and realistically apply them to your lifestyle, you can enjoy the fulfillment that they bring. However, it's easy to start off on the wrong track, as two other women explain:

Kim

"Since I don't have children, I wasn't sure how I would spend my days when I stopped working. I had plenty of ideas though, and was excited by the free time that I would have. I set out to try new experiences. First I enrolled in a continuing education program at our local college. I decided to take a few courses in architecture. I didn't know anything about the subject so I thought that I would begin by studying something entirely new to me. Then I went shopping with my last paycheck. Although I had never done any crafts, or sewn more than a button, I decided that this was the time to learn. I bought a shelf full of books to teach myself sewing, knitting, embroidery, needlepoint, and quilting. I bought patterns, materials, needles, threads, yarns, and kits. I went home and marvelled at all the ways I could enjoy my new lifestyle.

After I attended five classes I decided that I didn't want to know anything more about architecture, so I dropped the courses. I did learn some needlepoint and embroidery, and even completed a few projects. But three years later, everything else is still tucked away in the closet. I think I should have waited until I had been home awhile before I tried to choose new activities. Your attitudes and interests can change after you adjust to being at home, so it would be better to wait and see what happens.''

Jan

''I like the outdoors, and my husband and I have taken fishing vacations for years. When I worked, I looked forward to the calm, peaceful hours that we spent on the lake. You can contemplate thoughts and ideas in a beautiful setting, and sometimes catch your evening dinner! I planned to fish fairly often once I had the free time, but it wasn't the same. Now that my life isn't as hectic, I need to find more active interests to enjoy. Fishing was a great way for me to escape, but now I don't have anything to escape from.''

Phyllis

''I enjoyed my job in advertising, but I always wished I could become more involved in community service. I decided that I would become more active once I stopped working. When I mentioned my interest to a few people at church, I was on several committees and projects before I knew what hit me. Then a friend asked me to do some work for the American Heart Association. Soon I was regularly helping there, and working with Meals on Wheels. After a while I was so busy that I considered going back to work for a break! Instead I stepped back and re-evaluated my activities. I eliminated some, and phased myself out of others. I am still involved in community service, but now I have learned how to say no.''

Selecting Interests

You want creative options that will give you an outlet for your abilities and prove satisfying and rewarding. Your choices should include items that provide a challenge, require learning, and demand an investment of your mental and physical energy. You may choose to develop a current interest such as writing, drawing, or music—or you may discover an entirely new, previously unthought of activity.

In order to select the options most suitable to your needs, spend some time examining your feelings. Here are some questions to ask yourself:

- How did you spend your leisure time when you were working?
- What do you enjoy doing?
- What are your strengths?
- What comes easy for you?
- What are your weaknesses? (They are the ones that you hesitate to write down.)
- Do you need to see the results of your efforts?
- Do you require recognition for the things that you do?
- Do you want to help others?
- Are you uncomfortable being a follower?
- Do you like to solve problems?
- Do you enjoy creating new ideas?
- Would you like to try new things?
- What talents do you have?
- What interests would you like to develop?
- Do you prefer a routine?
- Do you like to work with your hands?
- Are you a 'joiner'?
- Are you interested in community projects?
- Do you prefer family oriented activities?

List twenty things that you would like to do, no matter how trivial they may seem. Then study the list. How many have you done recently? How many have you never tried?

Once you examine your feelings you can match them with the many interests that may apply. You might try several different activities before you select one that you enjoy. Remember that these are interests for you, and your choices should be those that make you happiest. Here are some ways that other women enjoy spending their time:

At Home

- Read your favorite kinds of books, or possibly some on a topic that you know nothing anything about.
- Games—board, card, and computer games are always fun. Play old favorites, learn new ones, create your own.
- Photographs—develop your photographic skills. Build a family pictorial history.
- Write a letter to the editor, poetry, stories, articles, an essay on something that you believe in, critiques of movies and books.
- Trace your family tree. Create a history book of your family and its activities, interests, and notable (or not so notable) achievements.
- Enroll in home study courses.
- Crafts—sewing, needlepoint, embroidery, crewel, knitting, quilting, crocheting, decoupage, ceramics, macrame, shells, baskets, sculpting, pottery, jewelry design, paper cutting, etc.
- Collect coins, stamps, postcards, matchbooks, antique toys, miniatures, campaign buttons, etc.
- Study a musical instrument, or revive your interest in one that you had studied previously.
- Listen to music. Become an expert on the different kinds, styles, performers, and writers.
- Solve puzzles—word, crossword, jigsaw, mysteries.

In The Community

- Volunteer to assist at charitable events. You might

register entrants for a march, set up tables for a fund raising dinner, call and schedule volunteers, type, file, stuff envelopes and packets, or work to raise funds yourself.

- Help battered women, unwed mothers, runaway children, missing children in anyway you can.
- Become a scout leader, campfire girl leader, 4H leader, big sister, etc.
- Spend time at the local animal shelter, at a nursing home, or at a food pantry providing assistance as needed.
- Start a neighborhood or church newsletter.
- Drive cancer patients for treatment, or the elderly to church or their doctor appointments.
- Collect for a worthy cause.
- Record books for the blind. Read to underprivileged children.
- Demonstrate crafts at a local nursing home, mental health center, or youth center.
- Assist at the hospital. Volunteer to work in the gift shop, to deliver flowers and mail, to push a library and newspaper cart, or in any other way you may be needed.
- Offer your services to your favorite politician or political party. Prepare letters, stuff envelopes, canvass voters, pass out materials, run errands, etc.
- Assist at your children's schools. Accompany them on field trips, help in the classroom, become a playground or lunchroom assistant.
- Establish a service to telephone the elderly who live alone. A few minute phone call each day will provide a contact with the outside world, and the comfort of knowing that someone will notice if they become ill.
- Coach an athletic team.
- Visit shut-ins.
- Volunteer to help at a hot-line.
- If you know a second language, offer to help

immigrants make the transition to this country and/or assist them in learning English.
- Help the handicapped.
- Start a drive for something that's needed in your community.

Outdoors
- Hike, walk, jog, bicycle.
- Learn to identify flora and fauna, bird watch.
- Plant a flower or vegetable garden.
- Landscape your yard.
- Swim, scuba dive, canoe, fish.
- Horseback ride.
- Enjoy spectator sports.
- Participate in your favorite sport—join a team.
- Fly a kite.
- Sunbathe.
- Golf.
- Play tennis or badminton.
- Water ski, snow ski.
- Sky dive.
- Plan tours and sightseeing trips.
- Visit amusement parks.

Other
- Take lessons in something that interests you (piano, dance, foreign language, etc.).
- Visit the library.
- Attend lectures.
- Visit museums, exhibits, fairs, festivals.
- Start or join a prayer or bible study group.
- If you like to sing, join a singing group or the church choir.
- Check your local YMCA or City/County Recreation Departments. They often offer activities, some are especially designed for mothers with small children.
- Exercise.

- Bowl.
- Play racquetball.
- Visit friends.
- Sign up for college or adult education courses. some schools offer counseling programs to help adults readjust if they have been out of school for years. You may decide to complete your degree, work toward a Masters or Doctorate, or begin studying toward a new credential. Or you may simply enjoy the idea of taking a few courses in subjects that you find interesting. If you are homebound, many colleges are now offering courses by mail for college credit. Consult the State and private universities in your area for further information. If you would like to complete your degree, or get a good start toward it, there is another alternative to attending classes.
- The College Level Examination Program (CLEP) offers testing in several subjects such as history, literature, etc. You can use these tests to acquire credit hours through the knowledge you have gained through life experience. There are books available to help you prepare for the exams. Check with your local college or universities for further information.
- Begin or join a group to trade babysitting services. Two ways of doing this are through an organized play group or a child-sitting co-operative. Play groups are smaller and more informal. Usually 3 to 6 mothers with children of similar ages will take turns watching the children. One day you watch all of the children for a few hours, another day a different mother does the same. It is usually done one day per week, which means that if there are four other mothers involved, you will have four days with free time. If you decide to take part in such a group, clarify the following points: discipline, feeding, potty policies, vacations and holidays, cancellations and illnesses.

- A child-sitting co-op is larger and more structured. Generally they are set up on a point system—each time you sit you gain points, each time someone sits for you you lose points. Most co-ops have a leader to help resolve problems, and a secretary to keep track of the points. Sometimes these positions rotate within the group, other times the workers are paid in child-sitting points. Some of the items you will want to discuss are: Who arranges the sits? What is the policy for refusing/cancelling sits? What our the number of points per sit, and how are they computed? When do extra points apply? (Such as after mid-night, holiday sitting, etc.) Where will the sits take place? How are members screened? What is the payoff penalty if you leave the co-op?

Potential Money Making Outlets

- Tutor students.
- Buy gifts for busy executives.
- Create a reminder service to help forgetful or unorganized people remember birthdays, anniversaries, etc.
- Sell your creations from a favorite hobby.
- Serve as a consultant.
- Teach something you know. You might hold seminars for a small fee and share your area of expertise.
- Do market research.
- Do part-time work for your former employer, or offer to serve as a vacation fill-in.
- Edit or type manuscripts, term papers, etc.
- Learn to program computers and create customized programs.
- Do bookkeeping/accounting for small businesses.
- Sign up with a temporary help service, such as Manpower or Kelly Girl.
- Babysit.
- Sell products through home parties.

• House sit.

Here is how one woman turned her desire for world travel into a fun experience:

Sandy

"I have always dreamed of traveling around the world. However, it's not a financial possibility for many years, so I decided to bring the world to my home. I bought an inexpensive map of the world, and started— one continent at a time, one country at a time. Most have tourism bureaus in our country, and I wrote and requested travel information, as well as suggested reading materials to better understand customs, traditions, and history. I received some wonderful packets which I enjoyed reading. Then I went to the library where I requested the suggested titles, and the reference librarian knew of a few others. I read my way through each country—then tried to bring their atmosphere to our home. I checked out cookbooks specializing in the country's cuisine, and tapes of their music and language. I attended lectures, festivals, and programs whenever I learned of them. Then one day a week I would cook a meal from that country, play their music, and talk about its history and places of interest. At first my husband humored me, and the children were bored. But I was fascinated, and finally my enthusiasm caught on. Now they will ask questions, and even bring announcements about certain special programs that they see to my attention. When I am able to travel I will be familiar with these countries, and I think that will help me to appreciate them more. In the mean time, it has expanded my view of the world, and my respect for men and women that I had never heard of.

I'm sure this fascination will continue to absorb me for years to come—there's a lot of world left out there for me to explore!"

Should You Volunteer Your Services?

You've already concluded that the status and recognition you received in your career did not meet all of your needs. Sometimes your personal values can be more accurately fulfilled by performing tasks that have a positive social impact but no material rewards.

The spirit of sharing and co-operation is an American tradition. From barn raisings and quilting bees to disaster relief and the Peace Corps, we are always willing to assist those less fortunate than ourselves. When you work to help others you contribute your time and energy, and you may gain a new perspective on your own life. Many women have found volunteer service to be a medium for personal growth. The selflessness of volunteerism puts aside material and personal concerns and allows you an opportunity to make someone else's life more satisfying, or to make your community a better place to live.

Traditional homemakers have always been the backbone of volunteer work in their communities. During the feminist revolution they were scoffed at, their efforts dubbed pseudo-work, and they were accused of actually hindering the movement for equality. Feminists believed that such work kept women trapped in servile roles, and that because society grants more status to paid workers, volunteer work prevented them from gaining the power that an income would bring. Lastly, they believed that if volunteers refused to do the work, organizations would hire and pay others to do it, meaning more jobs and status for all.

Time has given us a new perspective on these attitudes. A bureaucracy cannot provide the same spirit and individual attention that a volunteer would give. Government and big businesses have moved away from social programs, leaving the greatest responsibility for them to the communities. An absence of volunteers did not result in new employment opportunities, but rather the end of many programs and services.

Most paying jobs are not consistently fulfilling, and many

exist for the sole purpose of additional corporate profits. To claim that working with disadvantaged children, helping the elderly, or planning community centers was not as important as manufacturing widgets or designing shopping malls was an insult to our national conscience. A willingness to help others without benefit of material reward should provide more esteem than a simple paycheck.

Women who volunteer today can contribute innovative ideas from their work experience to revitalize services in their community. They can pursue interests and provide satisfaction for more than just themselves. If you would like to volunteer your services, you should select activities that will suit your needs and personality. One person can work well with the elderly, another may feel much more comfortable with children.

Starting Your Own Business

More and more women are starting businesses of their own. From 1980 to 1982 the number of women who were sole proprietors of a business increased by 10%, while the number of male sole proprietors increased only by 1%. Companies owned by women now account for forty billion dollars in sales.

A business of your own is often the perfect solution. You can combine having a career and a source of extra income with control over your life at home. And who hasn't dreamed of being their own boss at one time or another? If you are considering the idea, but aren't sure where to begin (or if you should try), this chapter will help you by raising many questions that you should consider and offering practical suggestions from a current small business owner.

What are your expectations towards having a business? What are you hoping to gain from it (besides money)? How much time can you devote to it? Why does the idea appeal to you? (Because you can get paid for doing something that you enjoy? Because you hope to become very rich very quickly?) Once you have a better idea of what your ultimate objective is, it is time to examine your qualifications.

The ability to create a great product does not necessarily coincide with the competence to operate a small business. In the beginning you must be all things: Accountant, Saleswoman, Marketing Manager, Product Development Manager, Distribution Manager, Business Manager, Typist, Bookkeeper, Receptionist, etc. In addition, you must be able to track details in these various functions while continually maintaining the big picture in your overall view. Do you have enough experience and interest to handle all of these functions? It may help to create a resume for yourself, listing the skills that you believe will apply. Then try to examine it objectively. Would you hire yourself?

Once you've made the decision to give it a try, it is time to learn everything you can. Visit your library and research every available source. You need information on owning a small business, management, marketing, production, etc. Try and study what similar businesses have done. Why did they succeed or fail?

After you've accumulated your notes there will probably be a number of questions. Your local commercial banker spends a great deal of time with other small businesses. An appointment there may prove very informative. The Small Business Administration is also available to help budding entrepreneurs. Contact your local office and request a list of their pamphlets and brochures, then make an appointment. If your type of business qualifies they can assist you in everything from setting up to obtaining financing. Then visit the owners of businesses that retail a product similar to yours. Learn as much as you can about the industry from them. Ask: Where do they buy their products from? (Mail order catalogs, advertisements, salespeople, etc.) Do they buy from small companies such as yours? Are there conventions and trade shows coming up that you could visit? Magazines you could subscribe to? What is the standard discount they pay for their products? What do they think about your idea? Are they interested in carrying it?

Then contact potential producers of your product for estimates. It may not be easy to find one, try your telephone book under various headings, or ask your local chamber of commerce for suggestions. When you contact them, ask for: minimum order, estimates for production, what other costs are involved, the amount of time it will take to produce, and (if you won't have room at home) if they have warehousing/storage facilities—and cost.

At this point, you have some idea of what you are getting into. Now it's time to sit down and make a business plan. Don't feel that you aren't large enough to do so, a small business needs planning and direction even more than a large one does. As you make your plan consider: How much money will you need to produce your product? Where will it come from? What market is your product aimed at? Why will your customers want to buy it? How much will you charge for your product? How many will you produce initially? Who will you sell them to? How much can you spend to advertise and promote the product? Where and how will you do it? How long can you wait before you begin to show a profit? What are your long range plans and goals?

There is a high failure rate among small businesses, and you may lose all that you put into it. You must be organized, flexible, and willing to take that risk. Here are a few more questions to ask yourself before you begin: Is my idea realistic? Does it fill a need? Do I have the necessary skills? Do I have enough money? Can I afford the loss if it fails? Do I know enough about it? Are my husband and children supportive? Is this the right venture for me?

Lastly, you should present yourself as professionally as possible to as many people as possible. Impressive business cards and stationery will give you credibility, and separate you from shoe string operations that every buyer is wary of. Distribute your cards to everyone that you know. Place them on community bulletin boards, slip one in with your bills when you pay them. Let your name and your product be known to as many people as possible.

Whether your business succeeds or fails, at times it will require some serious decisions on your part. A few other women who started their own business provide some insights:

Laura

"I began designing and sewing children's dress clothing because I thought it was terribly overpriced with impractical materials and little variety of style. Soon I was designing and sewing for friends and other family members. I kept getting more business through word of mouth, and before I knew it I had more requests than I was able to handle. Soon I was spending more time than I care to think about doing bookwork and projects for other people, and had little time to spend with my children—much less make clothing for them! I could have expanded and sub-contracted some of the work, but I preferred to keep it small and simple. I had left the bank because I wanted more time for myself and my family, and those were still my priorities. The extra money has helped us to take nice vacations, buy a better car, and redecorate the house. That is all that I really want. If I would have expanded I would have had little time to or enjoy those extras, it just wouldn't have been worth it to me."

Jackie

"I had been creating my own floral designs for years, and I knew from the many compliments and offers that I'd received that once I left my job I could start a business selling my arrangements, It was exciting at first. I made up samples and took them to restaurants, executive offices, etc. I obtained several regular customers right away. Soon I was delivering my arrangements all over town, and receiving requests for party decorations, wedding arrangements, and more. I had my sister and my friend working feverishly to help me, and although I loved the recognition that my work received, I had little time to enjoy it. Soon I began to lose interest. What had been a fun and creative outlet was turning into grueling hard work. There were constant demands on my time, and when my sister decided that she didn't want to help any more I decided to call it quits. I could have replaced her, but I really didn't want to bother with it any more. I gave up my regular clients and stopped accepting any other assignments. I think I might give it a try again in the future—the extra income was nice—but I would do it on a careful, one assignment at a time basis, or not at all.''

Donna

''We ended up with a succcssful business, but we did it the hard way. We had an idea to publish several books and sell them by mail. We read what we could about the subject, but there wasn't much available in our area, and we didn't know who to contact to obtain more. The few leads we had didn't yield much information. We made several expensive mistakes, the biggest was spending more on poorly designed advertising and promotion than we should have. We received orders, but not nearly enough to cover our costs. We kept trying and through some round about ways we began to talk to other people who knew the business and received some sound advice from them. Eventually we discovered better distribution outlets, and a number of books, courses, and seminars to help small publishers. Now we're growing steadily-sometimes faster than we are ready for. It's been an incredible learning process, and I have to say it's easier to put in long hours at something that is entirely yours. But you have to be committed to your business before you begin, because there are many months where it seems every time you take one step forward, you take two steps backward.''

Finding A Balance For Your Interests

Balancing your home, family, and personal interests can be done, once you establish priorities. Over the years you may discover different outlets for your energy, each providing satisfaction at that particular stage. Here are the stories of a few other women:

Toni

"As a young girl I loved ballet, and I studied for quite a few years. A leg injury destroyed any dreams I had of a career, so I turned to business and worked for some time with a major manufacturer. When I decided to stay home with my daughters I thought it would be fun to teach them what I had learned. Soon, other women in the neighborhood were asking me to include their children. I charged a small fee, but it was primarily for fun. I wasn't developing future ballerinas, just teaching grace, discipline, and a love for dance. When my daughters grew older, I stopped the school. I started working with handicapped children, showing them different ways they could move with the music, and helping them to appreciate their capabilities. I enjoyed this immensely, and after many years I decided to return to school. I obtained a teaching degree, specializing in working with the handicapped. Although I completed my degree the same year that my grandson entered first grade, I felt as young as ever. When I think about it, I have had a wonderful life. I was able to stay with my children while they were growing, yet I always could enjoy the things that I loved doing."

Lynn

"One winter my three children had a succession of colds, flus, and other childhood illnesses. I would read to them for hours to keep them entertained, and soon I was tired of the same story lines. I began to write little tales for each child incorporating details and interests from their own lives. They loved it, and even as teenagers they continue to treasure those volumes of stories. When I stopped working our librarian asked me to help with a story hour for children. I began writing little tales that included people and places in our community that the children were familiar with. Then I was asked to visit an elementary school and talk to the students about reading. Soon I was creating anecdotes based on local and state history, and I would visit each school once a month and spend an hour telling stories. It has brought history to life for the children, and I especially love accompanying them on field trips to historical landmarks. I love researching creating, and telling the stories, but most of all it thrills me to know that I have helped inspire children to read more, and to create stories of their own.''

Establishing interests that stimulate you will help you to maintain your self-esteem and independence. You may discover more satisfaction and fulfillment than ever before. The most important point to remember is, no matter how busy you are, find ways to enjoy your life and to make it a more pleasant experience for those around you.

Let's Get Physical

Your lifestyle as a homemaker will be different from that of a career woman. You will be less active because your days will be less hectic. You metabolism will slow down and your body will burn fewer calories. You will need less food to maintain your weight, yet you may be tempted to eat more because you have more time to cook and to enjoy your food. It is easy to forget about your appearance when you are often alone. This section is designed to help you maintain a good attitude about the way you look. You may be aware of some of the ideas included here, but it can help to refresh your memory. You might have had a diet and exercise program while you worked, but that may change once you leave your job. It may not be as convenient to attend your exercise class now, or you may not have the extra money or transportation. It's time to start a whole new routine for a whole new you.

Beauty

How often do you think about your physical appearance? Do you think that you are attractive? Beautiful? Most women don't. We all have our own idea of beauty, and that idea usually includes a few attributes that we don't have. If you have green eyes you may wish they were blue. If you have a petite build you may wish you were tall and willowy. If you listen to interviews of women famed for their beauty, you will find that they too feel flawed. They might point out that their eyes are too close together, their mouth too large, or their feet too big—all attributes that you never noticed because of the impression of beauty you received from them.

Beauty is more than an up-to-date hairstyle, the right eyeshadow for this season, and stylish clothes. It is more than a combination of physical attributes. It is an overall impression of appearance that combines body, hair, make-up, clothing and mental projection. You may have had little time to consider your appearance while you were working. You just checked to make sure that the parts fit together correctly in order to make the right impression, and dressed to fit the role that you were fulfilling. Now that your re-examining your values and taking a long hard look at your identity, your physical body will command more of your attention.

The mind is amazing. It can affect not only the way you treat yourself, it can also influence the way that others treat you. If you feel beautiful, you will look beautiful. If you tell yourself that you are lovely and attractive before you walk into room, it will help others to think of you as lovely and attractive too. Think of someone you know who is beautiful. What makes her that way? Does she really have perfect features, or does she project a glow or an image that is pleasing and attractive? She believes that image, and her confidence influences the way that others perceive her.

Inner beauty is important too. The older you get, the more your character becomes ingrained on your face. Do you frown a lot? Pout? Wrinkle your nose? In time these expressions will leave lines on your face that shape its appearance. Women who are tranquil and at peace with themselves will project that calm appeal to others.

If you have a poor image of your body you may put off things you would like to do with your life until you lose those pounds. And if you put it off, you will probably gain more weight. Soon you will find yourself stuck in a catch-22 . . . with no way out and little self-confidence to dig yourself out. If you dislike the way you look it may depress you, impair your sexual enjoyment and cause you to avoid social activities. Lastly, you can turn your body image into reality. Studies show that thin women who continually think of themselves as fat are more likely to gain weight. In the same vein, if you see yourself as thin when you are overweight it can help you to shed pounds.

Discipline is also part of beauty. Women who keep themselves attractive consider it important enough to force themselves to keep at it. Most of them have to work just as hard at it as you do, but you only see the end result. It becomes such an integral part of their routine that they may even respond "Oh, I don't do very much" when you ask them. If you know the details you would learn that they crave chocolate cheesecake or hot fudge delights or a gallon of mashed potatoes, but they manage to walk away from them. Or that they are just as busy and just as tired as you are in the morning, but they manage to keep an exercise routine.

You are just as important and just as wonderful as you were when you had a career. Concentrate on your appearance so that you will maintain your self-confidence. Spend time looking at fashion magazines, and at the latest hair and makeup styles. You don't have to run right out and try them, but they can help inspire and motivate you to continue your beauty routine.

Body Image

Here are some questions to ask yourself as you consider your feelings about your physical appearance:

- How would you describe yourself to a stranger?
- How do you feel about your body?
- What do you do to reinforce the problem?
- If you feel flabby, do you exercise?
- If you feel overweight do you cut back your eating to lose it?
- How do your feelings about your appearance stop you from doing what you want to do?

- Are you afraid to wear certain clothes? Go to the beach? Visit old friends?
- Do you avoid going out among strangers?
- Do you hide when you are in a room full of people?
- What can you change about yourself today—that can help you begin a new attitude of respect for yourself?

In a time when you are making a tremendous life adjustment from career to homemaker, you need all of the positive reinforcement you can get. It's very difficult to feel positive if you don't feel good about the way that you look. It isn't easy to start. Most of us lead busy lives, and it may not seem that you have time to worry about your appearance. Perhaps you've recently had a baby and you are too exhausted to care. Set small goals, then each little triumph will help to keep you going. Promise yourself something special when you reach your goal. What kind of goal can you set? It might be to lose weight, exercise more, fix your hair and put on makeup every day, dress up once a week, develop better dietary habits—whatever you would like to do to improve your life. It always helps to have the support of others as you begin. Your husband, a friend or relative might join you in setting a goal of their own and you can take turns helping to motivate each other.

Take charge and develop the right mental attitude. The more you try, the more you will want to try. Then you will look better, feel better and be happier. Isn't that the way you want to live?

Maintaining Physical Fitness

Fitness is a way of life combining your diet, your mental attitude and your activities. It's easy to procrastinate about keeping fit—a bowl of potato chips is simpler to prepare than carrot sticks. Reading a book takes less exertion than exercise. And there's always tomorrow—right? Wrong! If you don't keep fit it will harm you. Too much weight can cause stress on your bones, and lead to other problems such as heart disease, diabetes, osteoarthritis, or high blood pressure.

Nobody decides to gain weight or lose their shape. The pounds usually compound over time. An extra muffin at breakfast, or an extra candy bar in the afternoon all add up in time. Just 100 calories a day can put on ten pounds in one year! Weight loss usually takes time. It occurs in a stepping stone pattern, and the results will not show up right away. Each level maintains plateaus for a time before descending further. The plateau is the body's way of achieving balance as it readjusts to the changes being made.

Your metabolism determines the rate that calories are burned from the extra food you have eaten. This 'burn rate' is dependent upon your body size, activity and age. To lose weight you must speed up your metabolism by burning calories more quickly. The best method for this is exercise. You must also take in fewer calories because when you eat more than your body needs, the rest is converted to excess fat. You must cut out 3,500 calories from your food intake to lose one pound.

Yet it is very hard not to eat. We are tempted by delicious food in restaurants, grocery stores, even television advertisements. We reward ourselves with food. We find excuses to eat. Here are some of the most common justifications:

- I work hard.
- No one understands me.
- I'm so tired, I need the instant energy.
- Food makes me happy.
- I deserve to eat what I want after the day I've had.
- It's something to do when I'm bored.
- It helps me to forget my troubles.
- I eat when I'm angry. (So why take it out on yourself?)

If you know that your attitudes toward eating often encompass such justifications, try to overcome them by imagining them ahead of time. If you know you're having a hard day—think before you head for the kitchen. What else could give me satisfaction? Try to find alternative ways to alleviate those feelings. Would a nice bath be just as enjoyable? A visit with a friend?

When you decide to lose weight, don't bother with instant weight loss plans. Doctors say you should never try to lose more than five to eight pounds per month. Anything more can affect the skin's elasticity, and lack of elasticity is what causes wrinkles—who wants more of those? Plan your diet as you would any other goal in life. You know that you have self-control and discipline in other areas—apply them to your physical well being.

- Set a clear goal.
- Make a definite plan.
- Don't think of what you won't be able to do.
- Concentrate on the enjoyable aspects of being fit.

There are so many methods and ways to lose weight, that it can be overwhelming just to consider it. Diet books flood the market, and each seems to have its own system. Sometimes it helps to visit a nutritionist to receive a personally adapted program. Make sure of the credentials that this person has before trusting them with your diet. They should have a degree from an established university. Diuretics and sweaty heat treatments cause you to lose water, but you will gain it back as soon as you drink more. Skipping meals can cause you to overcompensate later. The best way to lose or maintain weight is to combine a healthy diet with exercise. There is no magic formula other than that.

How much should you weigh? Height and weight charts give varying ranges of weight depending on build and other factors. The best way to tell is body fat. How much excess can you pinch? The area above the hips is a good checkpoint. How many calories do you need? To maintain your present weight, multiply your weight times 15. To determine your calorie intake to lose weight, multiply your ideal weight by 12. That should be your daily calorie intake. **Before you begin any diet or exercise program contact your doctor first. If you are not healthy, smoke, don't eat right or have other problems you can die or become seriously ill if you follow the wrong program.** Don't use a checkup as an excuse not to begin, use it as a catalyst to start.

The Right Foods

I have a confession to make. Whenever I read diet books or magazine articles I always skip the sections that tell you about nutrition. I want to get right to the part that tells you how you can lose ten pounds in seven days and still eat all of your favorite foods. But in researching this book I learned many important facts that can help you to lose weight, maintain your weight, or keep you from gaining weight just by watching the foods that you eat. I also learned how dangerous certain foods can be to your overall health. New discoveries are being made every day and there may be changes since the last time you paid attention to such information (Was it in home economics?). The sections below aren't long and they are worth the time it will take to read them. Since there is no magical diet to skip over to, take the time to learn about nutrition here.

A balanced diet should include no more than 12-14% (44 grams per day) of protein, no more than 35% in fats, and the rest in carbohydrates (100-110 grams a day). What exactly are these dietary building blocks?

Protein is important to your body. It helps to build blood, muscle, skin and hair. But your body has to work harder to get energy from protein and it is high in cholesterol. If you eat a lot of foods that are high in protein it can increase your risk of contracting cancer and heart disease. Foods that contain large amounts of protein include:

milk	eggs	cheese
meat	poultry	fish
nuts	beans	grains

Fats are needed by the body to absorb certain vitamins, protect the nerves, and help the reproductive organs to function. But we need very few fats in our system, and most of us take in far more than we need in our normal daily diet. Fats are the most concentrated source of calories among all foods, and they require the fewest number of calories for the body to process them. Foods that contain a heavy amount of fats include:

cheese	ice cream	sauces
whole milk	yogurt	lunch meat
sausage	bacon	beef
egg yolks	cream	butter
oils	nuts	olives
chocolate	potato chips	hot dogs

Cut fats from your diet by eating more veal, poultry (without skin), and white fish than beef, lamb and pork. Use skim milk and eat other dairy products made from skim milk. Learn to enjoy your food steamed, baked or broiled instead of fried.

Cholesterol can build up in your blood vessels and prevent blood and oxygen from getting to your heart. This may eventually result in a heart attack. Limit your cholesterol intake to 300 mgs. a day.

This list of the cholesterol content of some foods was taken from "Cholesterol and Your Heart" (one of the many helpful guides you can obtain from the American Heart Association chapter near you):

1 cup	whole milk	33 mg.
1 cup	skim milk	4 mg.
1 oz.	cheddar cheese	30 mg.
1 Tbls.	butter	31 mg.
3 oz.	lean beef	77 mg.
3 oz.	beef liver	372 mg.
3 oz.	lean pork and ham	80 mg.

3 oz.	poultry (skinless)	82 mg.
3 oz.	fish	43 mg.
½ cup	lobster	90 mg.
½ cup	shrimp	96 mg.
1 med.	egg	274 mg.

Carbohydrates come in two types called *simple* and *complex*. They provide sugar as fuel for the brain and other muscles to work. Some carbohydrates are required each day for a balanced diet. Complex carbohydrates help you to keep from getting hungry by keeping your blood sugar level from dropping. Foods that include complex carbohydrates are beans, pasta, vegetables, rice, whole grain cereal and bread.

Simple carbohydrates cause a rapid rise in blood sugar, but it also drops very quickly. Foods that contain simple carbohydrates include sugar and fruits.

In summary, eat a healthy well-balanced diet from the four main food groups each day. Cut out as many fats and sugars as possible and eat more whole grains, fruits and vegetables.

Diet Tips
Here are many ideas for losing weight and keeping it off:

- It's easier to lose weight if you know your eating habits. Keep a food diary for a week or two. Write down everything that you eat, where and what time you ate it, and what made you decide to eat at that time. You may be surprised to discover how often you snack. Food eaten quickly is often forgotten.
- Examine your eating patterns in your diary. Are you snacking at certain times of the day? Try to be busy doing something else during those times.
- Curb cravings for sweets by eating something sour, such as a pickle.
- Make a list of all the benefits of losing weight . . . from wearing a smaller size to impress-

ing your old co-workers.

- Don't think about how long it will take you to lose weight. You will only get discouraged. Remember, if you do nothing it may get worse. Take action, even if it is in small steps.
- Spend time daydreaming about how you would like to look. Imagine yourself as clearly as possible. It will help you to project a new inner image.
- Put up pictures around the kitchen of how you looked when you were at your ideal weight, or of models who resemble the way you would like to look. They will serve as reminders of your goal.
- Reward yourself when you do well, but don't do it with food. There is nothing worse than the trap of ''I lost five pounds so I'll celebrate with five banana splits''. Buy yourself a necklace, a new outfit, a video, a book. Use the money you would have spent on junk food.
- If you slip, don't give up. Just pick yourself up and start again. There wouldn't be so many diet books around if everyone could go on a diet and stick to it.
- Put a gold star on your calendar for every day that you do well. It can help to show you how well you are doing—or haven't done. It may motivate you to try harder.
- Keep track of your progress. Write down your beginning weight; and your ideal weight. Check your status often.
- Remember, if you cheat, the only one that you hurt is yourself.
- Don't set unrealistic goals. Build toward them slowly.
- Do you want to lose ten pounds? Carry around a ten pound sack of potatoes every time you feel like eating. It's a good reminder of how much ten pounds is.
- Eat larger meals earlier in the day to allow yourself more time to burn off the calories.

- Lunch might be your most important meal. It controls afternoon energy—the time most people are tempted to snack. Eat a good combination of carbohydrates and protein.
- Learn to concentrate on your food. Set a place at the table every time you eat. Decorate it nicely. Don't read or watch television. This practice will help you to learn to avoid snacks. If you eat your food slowly, it will also help to curb your appetite during the meal.
- Try not to eat alone. Food becomes more of a comfort and solace than a nutritional source when you do. You also tend to eat less when you are around other people.
- Pay attention to what you eat. When you grab something, ask yourself "Do I really want this?" If you don't, you may find yourself back in the kitchen in a half an hour looking for something else.
- Find other activities for your hands. If you usually snack while you watch television, try knitting, crocheting, or needlepoint instead.
- Keep track of your progress. Plan for lapses. Set a time limit on how long you will allow yourself to cheat before you begin your diet again.
- If you feel you must eat something, force yourself to wait at least fifteen minutes. During that fifteen minutes, do something else. Start a load of laundry or work a crossword puzzle, when you distract yourself you may forget about eating.
- Don't expect weight loss to solve all of your problems, see it as something that you are doing for your own self-esteem.
- Put your food on smaller dishes. Or on one dish. It will make the portions seem larger.
- Keep busy and active. The less time you have to think about food, the less you will eat.
- Don't buy foods that you have trouble resisting. Keep any temptations out of sight. Stay out of the kitchen

as much as possible.
- The best diet is to eat the foods you enjoy, but to minimize your intake.
- Budget your calories to allow for parties, evenings out, holidays and weekends when you might eat more.
- Try munching a few crackers half an hour before meals to reduce your appetite.
- Stop eating before you feel full.
- Avoid wearing loose fitting clothing, it is harder to notice the extra pounds that way. If you feel uncomfortable in tight slacks, you are less likely to eat.
- When you crave a certain food, try eating it in your mind. Take yourself through it step-by-step. Surprisingly, it can satisfy your urge.
- Try cutting your food into smaller pieces.
- Encourage conversation at meals. Yu will eat less when you talk.
- Chew gum while you are preparing and cleaning up meals. You will be less likely to snack.
- Don't clean your plate if you are full. Starving children aren't going to get the leftovers if you don't eat them. If you are that concerned, make smaller portions and send the money you save to charity.
- Drink water or eat salads before meals. It will help to fill you up.
- Remember to consider all ingredients when you count calories (butter in cooking, milk in cereal).
- Watch for hidden sugar in foods such as canned vegetables, catsup, or frozen dinners.
- Limit or cut out alcohol. You are ingesting empty calories.
- Even low calorie meals can cause you to gain weight if your portions are too large.
- Substitute: Low calorie margerine for butter, baked potato for fried, boiled egg for scrambled, pretzels or

crackers for potato chips, jello instead of ice cream. All have fewer calories.

- If you crave foods such as sugar, salt and chocolate right before your period, eat more complex carbohydrates, make sure you are taking in enough vitamin B-6, and exercise.
- Caffeine (coffee, tea, soda pop) stimulates the appetite. You don't want your appetite *stimulated*, do you?
- Your body needs water. Drink when you are thirsty, especially if you are exercising. It helps to avoid dehydration and keeps your energy level high. The more salt you allow in your diet, the more water you should drink.
- Keep a relish tray in your refrigerator with carrot and celery sticks, apples, cauliflower, or whatever you enjoy. Then it will be readily available when you crave something to eat.
- Allow yourself a small treat every once in a while to avoid feeling of deprivation. But learn to stop at one—piece of pie, ice cream cone—or you will be right back where you started.
- When you are going to a party, fill up on low calorie foods before you go so that you less likely to snack.
- What about dining out? Most fast foods are high in calories, so try the snack bar available in most franchises. In restaraunts try to avoid looking at the menu and tempting yourself. If you must look at the menu, just look at the salad and entree section. Order first so that the selections of other diners won't tempt you. Ask them to remove the bread basket, or keep it on the other side of the table.

Crash Diets

Losing weight quickly is the most appealing way to shed pounds. No one wants to struggle through months of hard work if they can find an easier way. However, there are several problems with crash diets. They include:

- They may not work at all.
- You will probably regain whatever weight you lost.
- Some doctors believe that they lower the body's metabolic burn off rate.
- Fad diets are often imbalanced, and can cause malnutrition and other serious harm.
- Losing weight quickly and then regaining it, causes undue stress on the body.

I never paid much attention to doctor's warnings about fad diets. A few years ago a popular diet came out that promised quick weight loss as well as ways to keep it off forever. The diet recommended odd combinations of foods as well as large quantities of fruit, and assured readers that for the term of the diet it was nutritional. Of course it carried the standard warning to consult your doctor first—but I ignored it. I started to diet, and it went along very well. I lost 5 pounds the first week and 6 the second. By the third week I barely had energy to move, started having nosebleeds for the first time in my life and began to have terrible dizzy spells. I stopped the diet and went to the doctor. He told me that I should have known better . . . and I should have! I was looking for an easy way out, and could have become seriously ill instead. The point is—do not go on any diet that does not follow proper nutritional requirements. You may end up with more problems than just being overweight.

A Healthy Body
What if I told you that there was something that would:

- Help you to lose weight.
- Decrease your appetite.
- Burn calories more quickly and for longer periods.
- Help you to avoid wrinkles.
- Help you to ease stress and blow off steam.
- Give you healthier lungs and heart.
- Tone your body and take off unwanted inches.

- Help you to sleep better.
- Give you inner tranquility.
- Provide more balance in your lifestyle.
- Build stronger bones and more flexible joints.
- Aid your digestion.
- Give you a feeling of achievement.
- Give you more energy than before.
- Help you to live longer.
- Build your endurance.
- And will only take twenty minutes a day?

After discussing the pitfalls of fad diets it may seem that I am contradicting myself with such an all-encompassing list. You probably have already guessed that these benefits are the proven result of exercise. We hear about it all the time. In fact, our world seems to be divided between those who shout the joys of exercising from the rooftops; and those who think it's probably a good idea, and will start a program someday. According to Dorothy Schefer (Vogue 4/85) "The numbers add up and they're impressive: 75 million people exercising, 26 billion dollars being spent on fitness. But numbers mislead. Of those 75 million people only ⅓ are exercising to fitness."

The truth is many of us start programs with high hopes that fizzle away when other distractions occur. Health clubs report a huge dropout rate, equipment for jogging, tennis, or bicycling sits unused most of the time in homes across the country. We know exercise is good for us, but:

A. We don't have the time.
B. We don't have the energy.
C. We don't want to know how out of shape we really are.
D. We don't know where to begin.
E. All of the above.

It's hard to begin exercising, and it's even harder to keep at it. Yet, what other project could you do each day that could give you so many benefits? You deserve the time to improve your life, and there is no better time to begin than now. You may not think you have the time, but wouldn't you spend twenty minutes to help a friend? To make an extra trip to the store? To watch a television situation comedy that ultimately bores you? Inactivity does more than burn less calories. It causes fat to build, muscles to slacken and lethargy to set in. Make exercise a fun way to start the day. Put on your favorite music and move to it. If you just practice your dance steps you'll still be doing something to get yourself going. Eventually, you may decide to try a more beneficial routine. Here are some important points to remember when exercising:

- Don't invest in a lot of equipment until you are sure which type of exercise program you want to follow.
- Don't over-exercise or push yourself too far, too fast. It can cause serious injury.
- Too much perspiration can lead to dehydration and the loss of salt and minerals. Replace the loss by eating bananas or oranges.
- If you take medication such as high blood pressure medicine, consult your doctor. Some medication can alter your heart rate.
- If you feel chest pain, sudden dizziness or extreme breathlessness while exercising, stop at once and contact your doctor.
- Take extra care on warm, humid days to avoid heat exhaustion or heat stroke. Drink plenty of liquids. Signs of these problems include: sweating stops and your body temperature becomes very high.
- Wait two to three hours after eating a meal to exercise. Don't eat for about twenty minutes after you have exercised.
- Stop exercising if your muscles begin to ache or cramp.

- If you have just had a baby, start slowly with a few toning exercises. Consult your doctor first for suggestions.

Types Of Exercises

Some exercises help your heart and lungs, others help to tone muscles. Vary your type of workout for overall fitness and to keep from being bored. Some people enjoy exercising alone, others prefer the support of a group. You can find groups at your local health club, local YMCA or YWCA, and the park department in many cities that sponsor various programs. Before you join any exercise program, learn the teacher's credentials. Make sure that the workout area is on a padded surface to avoid injury. Don't select a program because your friends follow it, or because it is the newest "in" way for fitness. Do what you like to do.

As You Begin

Here are a few points to remember:

- Be sure to do warm up exercises for five to eight minutes to avoid injury and excessive strain.
- Your weekly program should include aerobic activity for twenty minutes four times a week or thirty minutes three times a week.
- When you have finished aerobic activity, walk around slowly to cool down and allow your heart and respiratory systems to return to normal.
- Be careful if you exercise to a record, cassette tape, video or television program. Don't try to keep up with the instructor at first, and try the positions before you begin. Make sure that you are not over straining or throwing your body off balance.
- Breath normally, many people hold their breath when they exercise which only adds to the strain on the body.
- Give your body time to adjust to each level of

exercising before you increase your activity. Stay at each level for at least two weeks.

- Remember, your muscles will not hurt until one or two days after the workout, so don't overdo simply because you feel okay. Always remember that the length of activity is more important that the amount of exertion.

Aerobic Exercise

We hear so much about aerobics today. Exactly what does the word aerobics mean? According to Doctor Kenneth H. Cooper, author of "Aerobics" (1968 M. Evans), aerobics are "any excerise that is of such duration and intensity that it requires the body to use extra oxygen, making the heart and lungs work harder . . . Aerobic exercise benefits the heart, lungs, and vascular system: The lungs process more air with less effort, the heart grows stronger and pumps more blood with each beat. Consequently, the blood supply to the muscles improves and total blood volume increases. In short, there's an improvement in the body's capacity to bring oxygen to the cells, where it combines with food to produce energy." (Ladies Home Journal, 4/85)

Combined with a healthy diet, aerobics may be the best possible way to lose weight. However, you should never exercise more than your heart can withstand. The best way to know is to find your target rate. According to the American Heart Association: "You can find out how hard to exercise by keeping track of your heart rate. Your maximum heart rate is the fastest your heart can beat. Exercise above 75% of the maximum heart rate may be too strenuous . . . exercise below 60% gives your heart and lungs little conditioning." (from "Exercise and Your Heart") Because your maximum heart rate can be affected by age and condition it is a good idea to contact your doctor before you begin an aerobic program. You can find your maximum heart rate by subtracting your age from 220. Never exercise at the maximum rate. Your target heart rate (what you want to build up to) can be found by taking your pulse after aerobic exercise for six seconds, then multiplying the number of beats by ten. That is your heart rate for one minute.

Choosing A Routine

Select an aerobic activity that has a variety of movements and tempos. The benefits you receive will depend on the amount of energy that you put into it. Aerobic exercises include:

brisk walking	jogging	running
cycling	swimming	jumping rope
dancing	cross country skiing	

Aerobic dance: A good program tones and shapes the entire body because it uses all of the muscles. Dance in tennis shoes to avoid possible injury.

Brisk Walking: You have to walk fast enough and long enough to receive aerobic benefits (at least twenty minutes), but this can be the best exercise program to begin with. Walkers are less likely to give up their program and you don't need special equipment (except for a pair of good shoes) . . . and you can do it anywhere. When you walk, stride from heel to toe, and carry as little with you as possible so that you won't be weighed down or thrown off balance.

Jogging: You should talk to your doctor before you begin to jog. If you have heart problems or a family history of heart disease you can kill yourself. You must do it properly and in moderation or it can put stress on the heart, the bones and your joints. Be sure that you dress properly: In the winter you would wear one less layer of clothing than normal and a hat to keep heat from escaping through your head; and in the summer you would wear light clothes to avoid dehydration from too much perspiration. Be sure to invest in good running shoes and when you run land on your heels—not the balls of your feet. Jogging is good for cardiovascular endurance, muscle strength, balance and flexibility.

Swimming: This is a fun way to exercise and the buoyancy of the water puts less stress on your joints. Swimming tones the upper body, stomach and legs and is good for the lungs.

Cross Country Skiing: This method is good for the arms and the legs. It builds endurance and balance and it burns the most calories of all exercise routines.

Bicycling: If you want the aerobic benefits you can't just roll along on a ten speed, you have to peddle against resistance. You can spend less time exercising on a stationary bicycle because you will not glide. Bicycling does wonders for the legs and hips.

Other Forms Of Exercise

For best overall fitness you should combine aerobics with muscle toning exercises. For instance, if you bicycle, tone your muscles from the waist up.

Calisthenics: These movements include commonly known exercies such as situps and leg lifts. They help to tone and shape specific areas. However, many people feel that they are boring and they are the most likely form of exercise to be dropped. Use them to complement other exercise programs.

Weight Lifting: You don't have to develop bulging muscles if you lift weights. Moderate weight lifting can tone and trim the body and help you to lose inches instead of pounds.

Of course there are many other activities that burn energy and can be a fun way to keep in shape. They include:

Dancing: Jazz, tap, ballet and ballroom dancing are popular forms of exercise. They use the body, develop rhythm and balance, and can be fun. Start with a basic class and be sure to do warm up exercises first. Many videos are now available to provide instruction for dance steps.

Racket sports: Tennis, squash and racquetball are enjoyable sports, but they do not build cardiovascular endurance. Be sure to do warm-up exercises first and wear well-cushioned shoes.

Other: There are many other activities that provide

challenge, toning and miscellaneous benefits. They include: basketball, baseball, soccer, bowling and horseback riding.

Burning Calories

If you want to select the activities that will burn the most calories quickly, here is a chart that provides information to give you an idea of what amount of movement is needed. The following information is quoted from the American Heart Association booklet "Exercise and Your Heart":

"The calories spent in a particular activity vary in proportion to one's body weight. For example, for a 100 pound person reduce the calories by ⅓, for a 200 pound person, multiply by 1⅓ . . . A lighter person burns fewer calories, a heavier person burns more. The following chart provides the number of calories burned per hour by a 150 pound person:

Activity	Range	Calories Per Hour
Bicycling	6 mph	240
Bicycling	12 mph	410
Cross Country Skiing	1 hour	700
Jogging	5½ mph	740
Jogging	7 mph	920
Jump Rope	1 hour	750
Run in place	1 hour	650
Swim	25 yds. per min.	275
Swim	50 yds. per min.	500
Tennis	Singles 1 hour	400
Walk	2 mph	240
Walk	3 mph	320
Walk	4½ mph	440

After You Have Begun

Because most of us lose weight in certain places first (such as our face or our breasts), it may be frustrating to wait for the loss of inches where we desire them the most. But exercise helps the body to redistribute fat, and in time it will start to disappear in those other places too.

Once you reach your target weight, set limits on yourself. For example: Whenever you gain three pounds, or a certain outfit feels tight, promise to reduce your calorie intake and increase your activity to take those unwanted pounds off before they become a problem. Remember that to maintain your body's weight you must only take in as many calories as it requires. Increase your food intake slowly. One pitfall of successful weight loss is that once you achieve your goal you can become over-confident and fall back into your old eating habits. Give away your larger-sized clothes so you will have nothing to wear if you gain weight; watch what you eat and remain active; and you will be able to enjoy good physical fitness for years to come.

Managing Your Time

With few tasks to accomplish each day and unlimited time to complete them in, it is easy for the days to slip by while your work is left undone. As a homemaker, it is essential that you systematize your day, and organize your projects. If you insist on handling problems and interruptions as they occur you may discover that there is little time left for you to pursue the interests you have looked forward to.

Without a plan or priorities your days will lack purpose and direction. Unless you set ground rules you may find them cluttered with too many demands on your time. How many hours will you devote to advising and helping others? When should you say no to requests for your assistance? If every day is a hectic one, you may easily fall into the trap of assuming that a great deal of activity is proof of how much you are accomplishing. Yet continuous activity is no indication of productivity. Chaos is not a synonym for spontaneity. Unless you control your time, you may find that you have little freedom to participate fully in your own life. And unless you respect your schedule, no one else will. You certainly don't want to find yourself just as frazzled and overtired as you were when you were working, but without the income and prestige!

When you are raising small children it can be extremely difficult to establish any type of time management. Your routine is constantly interrupted with minor mishaps or needs for attention. Because a daily list or schedule can seldom be completed in these cases, the best way to organize is to set small, very flexible goals each day. If you lower your expectations of accomplishment, you lower your chances of continual frustration. One mother further illustrates the point:

Peggy

"Life at home is very different from the workplace. You usually have some type of routine on your job, and although meetings, clients, or last minute projects can interrupt it, you know that tomorrow or next week things can return to normal. Here, the struggle never ends. My goal one day was to simply complete the grocery shopping, find a gift for my mother's birthday, and look for shoes for my daughter. Before it really began, I had picked up a box of cereal that had been thrown all over the kitchen f loor, wiped up seven spills, removed a stuffed bear from the toilet, and loaded the dishwasher, I managed to get us both dressed and to the mall, but as I was waiting to pay for my mother's gift my daughter needed her diaper changed. I had trouble finding the restroom, so we had a real mess. I cleaned her up and tried looking for shoes, but she was definitely ready for her nap. I took her home and put her to bed, then dashed around doing laundry and straightening up. I was able to sit down for ten minutes, then she was awake. We were both dressed and ready to go again when I was interrupted with a phone call. I was only distracted for a few minutes, but in that short period of time she managed to crawl into the kitchen, tip over the trash and redistribute it over herself and the kitchen. I cleaned everything up, changed her clothes, then got her in the car. Before we made it through the grocery store she got sick, and I had forgotten another change of clothes. I washed her in the restroom, and tried to hurry before I ran into anyone that I knew. We made it home, and I redressed her, put away the groceries and started dinner. It was a hectic and tiring day, but I was satisfied. We hadn't accomplished everything that I had wanted to, but more than I had expected to.''

Time is a valuable commodity. Because it is irreplaceable, each day should be treasured. You are not being controlled when you manage your time, you are gaining control of your life. Don't wait for the perfect day to arrive before you start your next project or begin a new routine. Do it now. Set a time limit for each of your tasks, and allow the important ones to receive more of your attention. Keep as near to your goal as possible. The reason is simple. If you have an entire day to complete two tasks, you will take the entire day to finish them. If you only allow two hours for their completion you will problably finish them in two hours Because most of us share this trait, the best way to control it is to set deadlines for ourselves.

Organization takes both discipline and commitment. The amount of structure that is necessary depends upon your personality. Some women enjoy a routine, and are most efficient when they use a detailed schedule with even leisure activities penciled in. Others are content with a mini-list of tasks that provide a semblance of routine for each day. For them, any more structure would be intimidating or ignored. Create an organization plan that will suit your own needs.

Daily Diary
Keep a daily diary for a week to discover how well you are utilizing your time. This effort will provide you with a detailed study of where and how you are expending your energies, and in what ways you should alter or adjust your routine. First break your day into fifteen minute segments, and write down everything you do, no matter how unimportant it may seem. Did you spend the last fifteen minutes trying to get your son to pick up his toys? Will you

spend the next fifteen minutes trying to locate your new shoes? You may be surprised to discover the amount of time that is spent on trivial details.

As you examine this diary, look for the portion of the day that you are most energetic and creative. If you save your most difficult tasks for those high energy periods you will accomplish even more.

Make A List

Make a list of your plans for each day. (Some find it easier to prepare one the night before.) If you are unorganized and need structure make it a very specific one and include leisure activities. Any schedule should include at least ten items, but don't make the list so long that it is intimidating.

Next, set priorities. Which items on the list are urgent? Important? What can be postponed or done when you have the time? By following your priorities you can be sure that you are accomplishing what is essential each day. Those chores that are not finished can be transferred to the next day's list.

What about items that must be completed in the future—next week or next month? A simple solution is to buy a calender that has plenty of room to write on, and hang it in a place where you will notice it often. When you think of a task or appointment, mark it on the calender. Note birthdays, anniversaries and other special occasions, with enough lead time to purchase gifts or cards before those dates. As you make your daily list, check your calender and add any tasks that are recorded on it.

Examine your list. What problems can occur that will make it difficult to complete the task? Are there any items that could be delegated? What tasks can be combined? (Such as folding laundry while talking on the telephone.)

Delegating Tasks

Your family may have been fairly independent when you had a career. That doesn't mean that they won't try to change things now that you are a full-time homemaker. If you are having difficulty obtaining everyone's full co-operation, the best thing to do is to put each problem in its proper perspective. When you were working and trying to motivate an employee to complete a task, you were well aware of the alternatives. They were:

1. You could ignore the task.
2. You could complete the task yourself.
3. You could induce someone else to complete the task.
4. You could spend your days reminding them to complete the task.

That same perspective can be applied to life at home. Obviously family members are not quite the same as employees (you can't fire them), but with proper guidance and motivation you can examine each problem with these principles in mind, and determine the best solution for yourself and your family.

How To Begin

There are times that you have so much to do, you don't know where to begin. If you feel overwhelmed, break each chore into smaller steps. Select a small job that you can do right now. By taking action you can eliminate any helpless feelings that you may have. It's best to start with something easy. If you have an entire room to clean, choose one section and complete it. Instead of tackling an entire closet, clean one shelf. Once you have one part accomplished, you will find that it is easier to complete the rest. Doing the tasks one step at a time will help you to slowly but surely reduce the workload.

Time Saving Ideas

Here are some other ideas to assist you:

- Have a place for everything, such as keys, shoes, and catalogs.

- Never allow housekeeping chores to overrun your life. Allot a certain amount of time to them each day, and leave the rest.
- Buy ahead. Keep stamps, birthday cards, and emergency dinners on hand to save unnecessary trips to the store.
- Use waiting time productively. Water plants while you wait for a television program to start. Write a letter while you wait in the doctor's office.
- Set limits. If there is a job that you have been avoiding, commit yourself to one hour a day on it until it is completed.
- Don't try to do everything yourself. Delegate.
- Do two things at once. Mend while you listen to the news.
- Don't procrastinate. Work can pile up and overwhelm you. A cavity that you ignore today can mean expensive and time consuming dental work later.
- You will never be able to do it all, so stop trying.
- Don't wait for a good time to start, just begin.

It's A
Wonderful Life

Each generation of women must surmount new obstacles and live up to the standards that they set for themselves. We have been fortunate. The struggles of previous women have allowed us to enjoy more choices and more opportunities than any generation in the past. Yet with the benefit of these options come new responsibilities. We have high expectations for ourselves. We want to use our special qualities to improve the workplace and the world around us. We have a chance to create an impact on the attitudes and opportunities for women in generations to come.

Our next step is to value the roles of all women equally. A doctor and a fireman are both vital at the time that they are needed. In the same way, a career woman and a homemaker are both essential in our society today. One can blaze new paths for women to positions in the higher echelons of business and government. The other can reinforce the stability of the home, and strengthen the family bonds by her continuous presence. The wonderful thing about being a woman today is that a woman can choose to live out both roles simultaneously, or at different stages in her life.

It is difficult to give up a successful career. If you have devoted your time, talent and energy to a job—it isn't simply a matter of just walking away. When you have made sacrifices and compromises, you can't let go without some effort. And it's always easier to leave your options open... to have a little bit of everything rather than taking a chance and making a mistake. Yet, if try to be everything that you believe you must be, you may discover that your life is without focus, direction or a true sense of your inner needs. You know what is best for you and your temperament, and where your priorities lie.

Some choices entail a tremendous amount of risk, and you may feel that this is one of them. There are few decisions that are irrevocable. You may not be able to resume the same career, but there are always new avenues to pursue. And whenever you take a chance you gain the opportunity to obtain new rewards and experiences. Remember, it is difficult to discover new satisfactions and freedoms when you are on a treadmill. Take a chance and put aside your hopes for immediate gratification and examine your long range goals. Take the time to listen to your inner voice.

As a homemaker you have time to grow morally, intellectually and spiritually. You can savor the experiences that make life enjoyable and create new options for satisfaction and fulfillment. Use your abilities to improve the lives of those around you. Make your home an example of love, nurturing and care. Teach your children to value people over material things. True success is living your life the best way that you can. You are your own source of happiness.

You can go home again. There is a world of freedom and leisure, happiness and satisfaction just waiting for you to step into it. And in the words of Jonathon Swift: "May you live all the days of your life."

Bibliography

American Heart Association, 1984, "Exercise and Your Heart" (booklet)

American Heart Association, 1984, "Cholesterol and Your Heart" (booklet)

Abarbanel, Karin, "Women Watch: Working Women Households", The Executive Female, March/April 1985

Berkowitz, Bernard, 1977, "How To Take Charge of Your Life", Harcourt Brace Jovanovich

Bozic, Patricia, "How To Ease Off Those Hard To Lose Pounds", Redbook, July, 1985

Brazelton, T. Berry, M.D., "You're Okay, They're Okay", Family Circle, 9/24/85

Cardozo, Arlene Rossen, 1976, "Woman At Home" Garden City, New York, Doubleday & Co.

Dusky, Lorraine, 1982, "How To Eat Like A Thin Person", New York, Simon & Schuster

Friedan, Betty, 1981, "The Second Stage", Summit Books (Simon & Schuster)

Goodman, Ellen, 1979, "Turning Points", Garden City, New York, Doubleday & Co.

Grant, Roberta, "The New One-Paycheck Family", Ladies Home Journal, 9/84

Groller, Ingrid, "The Women's Work Poll", Parents, 7/83

Henry Jeanne, 1980, "Mother To Mother Baby Book", New York, Avon Books

Hoffecker, Pamela Hobbs, "Will the Real Working Mom Please Stand Up?", Parents, 4/85

Hoke, James H., 1980, "I Would If I Could and I Can", Stein & Day

Houston, B. Kent, "Housewives Also Have Heart-Risk Rates", Associated Press, 8/28/85

Jacoby, Susan, "How 40,000 Women Feel About Their Jobs", McCalls, 1/85

Jones, Peggy, 1985, "The Sidetracked Sisters Happiness File", Warner Communications Co.

Keating, Kate, "How Is Work Affecting American Families?", Better Homes and Gardens, 2/82

Ladies Home Journal, "Women vs. Women: Report From the Front Lines", 8/82

Leedy, J.J., M.D., 1982, "How To Eat Like A Thin Person", New York, Simon & Schuster

Levine, Karen, "Mother vs. Mother", Parents, 6/85

Linde, Shirley Motter, 1976, "Now That You've Had Your Baby", New York, David Mckay Company, Inc.

Long, Charles, 1981, "How To Survive Without A Salary", Horizons Publ. Ltd.

Lund, Doris, "Pardon Me, But I Like Housework", Readers Digest, 12/84

Mansfield, Stephanie, "Career Women Who Drop Out", Chicago Sun Times, 3/24/85

Morical, Lee, 1984, "Where's My Happy Ending?", Addison Wesley Publishing Co.

Morse, Susan, "Superwoman's Not So Perfect Balancing Act", Chicago Tribune, 6/13/85

Newman, Mildred, 1977, "How To Take Charge Of Your Life" Harcourt Brace Jovanovich

Orth, Maureen, "Friends For Life", Vogue, April, 1985

Panter, Gideon M.D., 1976, "Now That You've Had Your Baby", New York, Dick McKay Co., Inc.

Peck, Ellen, 1975, "A Funny Thing Happened On The Way To Equality", Prentice-Hall

Reeves, Pamela, "Why I Quit", Parents, 7/84

Reice, Sylvie, "Health and Fitness Guide", Ladies Home Journal, 4/85

Rubin, Nancy, "Women vs. Women", Ladies Home Journal, 4/82

Seligman, Susan Meilach, 1980, "Now That I'm A Mother, What Do I Do For Me?", Chicago, IL, Contemporary Books Inc.

Sexton, Linda Gray, 1979, "Between Two Worlds: Young Women In Crisis', William Morrow & Co.

Schefer, Dorothy, "Fit For What?", Vogue, 4/85

Shaevitz, Marjorie Hansen, 1984, "The Superwoman Syndrome", Warner Books

Sherberg, Ellen, "Career Woman To Full-Time Mommy", Parents, 1/81

Sills, Barbara, 1980, "Mother To Mother Baby Book", New York, Avon Books

Stein, Harry, "The Case For Staying Home", Esquire, 6/84

U.S. News & World Report, "She's Come A Long Way—Or Has She?", 8/6/84

Wagner, Barbara, "The New One-Paycheck Family", Ladies Home Journal, 9/84

Young, Pam, 1985, "The Sidetracked Sisters Happiness File", Warner Communications Co.

Index

Other Titles From Bryce-Waterton Publications That You Will Enjoy:

It is always helpful to obtain fresh insight and guidance during important times of your life. These informative books are both practical and fun to read—an investment that will make your life easier. Order today—and don't forget your friends!

NEWLYWED: A Survival Guide
To The First Years Of Marriage

When one out of two marriages fails, how can a newly-married couple avoid divorce? By learning to identify the special problems they face during the crucial years of marriage, and laying the groundwork for a strong and lasting relationship. This book will help them to recognize problems before they occur, and take steps to make their marriage a successful one. Packed with ideas and advice for making everyday decisions concerning money, home, and family, **NEWLYWED** is an important first purchase for all married couples!

YOU CAN GO HOME AGAIN:
The Career Woman's Guide To Leaving The Workforce

Can a woman have a fulfilling lifestyle without struggling up the corporate ladder? This book will answer that question and more. Making this career choice is a big step, and today's woman needs to be prepared in order to adjust properly. While pondering her decision, she wonders . . . What would I do all day? Would I enjoy staying at home? Can I be 'just a housewife'? This informative book will deal with all of her concerns, and help her to make a smooth transition to a lifestyle with new and satisfying challenges. A must for every working woman.

THE GROOM TO GROOM BOOK

This unique guide for the bewildered groom-to-be will spark his interest in the wedding plans. Packed with advice from previous grooms, this practical and informative planner covers every topic from rings to receptions. Included are: A complete budget guide; planning timetable; legal/business affairs; charts; illustrations, and much more. Now, he can fully enjoy all of the wedding activities, and turn a hectic and emotional experience into a carefree celebration.

THE BRIDE TO BRIDE BOOK

Since its appearance on the wedding market, this book has become one of the most popular wedding planners available today! A complete wedding consulting service at an affordable price, this book is packed with practical ideas, money-saving tips, examples, illustrations, and worksheets that will help the bride-to-be avoid problems, save money, and make the right decisions for a perfect wedding day.

THE BRIDES THANK YOU GUIDE

Saying "Thank You" will be easy and fun with the help of our handy guide. It provides many helpful ideas, and over 75 examples and suggestions to make your job easier. You'll want to acknowledge each gift received, and show gratitude to those who helped make your wedding day a special one. It's not what you say, but how you say it, that means so much to the giver.

Order Form

Bryce-Waterton Publications
P.O. Box 5512, Dept. N
Portage, Indiana 46368

Please rush me the following books:

Newlywed .... $8.95 _____

Career Woman's Guide .... $9.95 _____

Groom-to-Groom Book .... $5.95 _____

Bride-to-Bride Book .... $6.95 _____

Bride's Thank You Guide .... $1.25 _____

Sales Tax (Ind. residents only)............... _____

Shipping* .... _____

Total enclosed** .... _____

**Check or money order in U.S. funds only.
  Price includes postage and handling.

Shipping: Add $1.00 per book for quicker 1st class mail
(No additional charge for Thank You Guide).

I understand that I may return any book for a full refund if
not satisfied.

Name: _____

Address: _____ Apt. _____

City & State _____ Zip _____